Enid Byford has had several careers – as a librarian (for which she trained upon leaving school), as a teacher of English in a Nigerian school, as a freelance writer/photographer in Singapore and Canada, and most recently as an editor – the last ten of seventeen years in Ottawa were as managing editor of *Canadian Geographic*. Since returning with her husband to Somerset at the beginning of 1984 she has worked as a freelance editor/proof reader and writer. Her most recently published book *Somerset Curiosities* (1987) is now in its second printing.

SOMERSET MURDERS

ENID BYFORD

THE DOVECOTE PRESS

First published in 1990 by The Dovecote Press Ltd
Stanbridge, Wimborne, Dorset BH21 4JD

ISBN 0 946159 76 9

© Enid Byford 1990

Photoset by Character Graphics, Taunton, Somerset
Printed and bound by Biddles Ltd
Guildford and King's Lynn

Contents

Introduction

This book is a compilation of some of the murders that took place in Somerset or were committed by Somerset people fifty or more years ago. Information came from many sources – Assize Records, Sheriffs' Reports, Coroners' Inquisitions, Gaol Records, Gaolers' Accounts (£2 for a hanging), Chaplains' Diaries, and from old issues of newspapers. The local press did not really get into the swing of producing verbose accounts until the middle of the nineteenth century and then some of the reports came as much from the reporter's lurid imagination as they did from court proceedings.

Some of the Gaol Records contain fascinating details about the accused; at different times the authorities obviously considered certain items of information important – for instance, some records note the educational standard of the prisoner – whether able to read and write (separate entry for each); the religious persuasion – more frequently left bare, despite the belief today that everyone attended some place of worship a hundred or more years ago; at another time the fact of whether the person was married and had children was recorded. All too often too little was noted of the crime of which the prisoner was accused – a laconic 'killed Mary Taverner at Bath on June 23 1857' can be most frustrating, especially when Joshua Sheen, an illiterate labourer aged 35, married with three children and three previous convictions was jailed for just 6 calendar months (with hard labour). One longs to know the mitigating circumstances that gave Joshua 6 months, and why the man who followed him into the dock at the same Assizes, one Frederick Davis, aged 18, also an illiterate labourer, received 5 years penal servitude for assaulting

Thomas Carey on June 6 and robbing him of a tobacco box, 2 half crowns and a shilling. Was Mary Taverner's life not worth more than 6 months – or was it possible that the judge, bearing in mind the cost to the parish of supporting Joshua's three children, decided upon leniency?

Most of the Assize Records (almost invariably thickly coated with dirt when brought up from the storage room) give little more beyond the name and sometimes the age of the accused, the charge, the names of the jury members, the verdict and the sentence, with a note as to when an execution was carried out. This sparseness made the wealth of material associated with the Mannings' murder trial all the more exciting. To be able to handle Exhibit 1 and see Frederick Manning's attempt at forging O'Connor's signature, to be able to read the transcribed accounts of the statements as made from the witness box, and to be able to read the words said by the accused, with no reporter's embellishments, was unforgettably thrilling.

On the whole Somerset people are, and have been, a law-abiding company. However, I was struck by the fact that on the whole our murderers (and their victims) were poor folk. Possibly because the wealthy had other means of getting at those who stood in their way (divorce, for instance, was a very costly business, and so a man – or woman — with very little money, might well have been tempted to take a permanent way out of a marriage); possibly also because those who didn't have to live cheek by jowl with an extremely irritating partner were better able to avoid – or shrug off – the petty annoyances that eventually led to murder in domestic situations.

Among the rich, though, we have had a few dyed-in-the-wool villains who tried to get others to do their dirty work for them, and in more than one case also paid with their lives. It speaks well for British justice that such men were not able to buy their way free (possibly because of the system of being tried by one's peers – none of whom would have been overawed by the rank of the prisoner standing at the bar).

It is interesting too, to note, that not every judge in the past automatically sentenced a murderer to hang; transportation for life, or possibly for a number of years was harsh, but it did at least give the prisoner a chance to make good elsewhere. The records available for Shepton Mallet Gaol cover much of the nineteenth century and yet very few murders resulted in the death penalty. Manslaughter at times was treated far more lightly than many other offences – William Barrett, an 18-year-old labourer, was arrested in June 1868 for the manslaughter on 23 May of Arthur Bush at Bath and received one week's hard labour at the Wells Assizes. Not quite so lightly treated was Susan Gardiner (a single servant, aged 34), who came before the same judge charged with attempting to conceal the birth of her male child (no mention of the child dying); she received a calendar month's hard labour. And from an earlier time, and particularly poignant, is the case of the 10-year-old boy convicted of theft and sentenced to hang at Bridgwater. As he mounted the scaffold, he is reported to have cried for his mother.

Of course, some of the murders were deliberately planned and cold-bloodedly carried out, but the majority of Somerset's murderers acted on the spur of the moment — and then there were a few others who had to pay the supreme price for a deadly mistake.

I apologise for the paucity of illustrations. I used to think, before I started on this book that the libraries would be filled with line drawings and steel engravings showing the murderers and their victims, but the newspapers of the mid-nineteenth century are singularly lacking in pictures, and apart from one or two pamphlets, notably *The crying Murther*, featuring the unfortunate Mr Trat, and Hunt's 1821 *Investigation at Ilchester Gaol*, artists' impressions of gruesome events and unpleasant personalities seem not to have survived.

Be that as it may, I hope the reading of these accounts will prove as interesting as the gathering of the material has been.

ENID BYFORD

Acknowledgements

I have spent many hours in reference libraries and records offices in an attempt to make this as accurate an account as possible, and am grateful to the staffs of the Public Record Office, London, Bridgwater Reference Library, and Somerset Record Office for their patient attention. David Bromwich of Somerset County Local History Library has been most helpful, digging out snippets for my information and old books that might give additional facts. I should also like to thank Mr F.G. Randle, formerly of the *Somerset County Herald*, and Mrs Gillian Allen of Wellington for the information they made available; Dr Robert Dunning and Miss Marie Siraut of the Victoria History for leading me to stories of the less well publicised cases and for reading the typescript and correcting errors (I have added some material since, so if there are mistakes they crept in during that time); and to David Burnett for copy editing and polishing before publication.

Finally, my husband, now nearing 83 years of age, should receive recognition for his sterling service in making endless cups of tea and coffee, without which this never could have been finished.

A FRONT VIEW OF ILCHESTER GAOL,

Drawn on the 2nd of May, when Duke Flower, of Bath, and John Kew, of Weston, were Executed.

1 2 3 4 5 6 7 8 8 9

The outside of Ilchester Gaol. Two corpses hanging from a gibbet are just visible above the entrance.

A PEEP into ILCHESTER BASTILE

A contemporary engraving of Ilchester Gaol.

1

The Sheriff's Goal at 'Ivelchester'

For some 700 years there was a gaol at Ilchester. Documents show that in 1166 the presence of the County Gaol conferred on Ilchester the status of a county town, confirmed by regular meetings of the shire and county courts. Ilchester thrived as a result. Then some time in the 1280s the courts were moved to Somerton; the economy began to decline and despite a reversal to the former venue in the 1360s, Ilchester never regained its old importance. The gaol was restored and re-established by 1371 and remained in place until 1843, with new buildings in Northover parish replacing the old four-teenth century ones in 1599.

Until 1811 executions took place outside the town at a field called Gallows Five Acres, on the west side of the Yeovil road about half a mile from the town. Large crowds used to attend the executions, which were times of celebration and ribaldry and were known as Hang Fair Days and contributed greatly to the town's economy.

The last Hang Fair Day was claimed to have taken place on 6 April 1835 when two apprentices, John Hore and John Howe, paid the penalty for killing John Harvey of Langport at Sandpits Hill on 7 March. The two men had attacked Harvey with his own soldering iron, then replaced it by putting a bloodstained rack stave near the body. The stave had been used as a walking stick by a neighbour who, having been overheard praising its potential as a weapon, was under suspicion of committing the crime. He in turn suspected the apprentices. Hiding under their bed one night, he heard them talking about the deed. Eventu-ally he moved, whereupon the apprentices confessed on the grounds that the Devil was heaving them out of bed.

The two miscreants were hanged on a drop built above the front lodge of the gaol, watched by the crowds who gathered on the river bank opposite. Those wanting to watch from a coal wharf immediately facing the gallows were charged 1/- each (at a time when the average weekly wage for a farm labourer was 6/-).

Three other men were executed at public hangings at a later date, but their deeds were more mundane and had less popular appeal — 18-year-old Daniel Case, the very last one, was hanged on 1 September 1836 for setting fire to a house.

During the 700 years of its existence, frequent outbreaks of typhoid fever occurred in the gaol, caused by the constant seepage from the privies into the wells that supplied the drinking water. In 1624 the house of correction was separated from the gaol and a section was reserved for women felons. The place was dank, and life for inmates was made especially unpleasant under the care of William Bridle, a notorious gaol keeper who held sway from 1808 until his dismissal in 1821.

All too many people spent their last days on earth at Ilchester – between 1810 and 1845 approximately 1,400 persons were executed for crimes that had ceased to be capital offences by the 1930s.

There were those who went to the gallows for murder, such was William Needs, aged 26 and born at Holcomb near Wiveliscombe. He was sentenced for his part in robbing John Pring of five and a half guineas in 1804. Robbery was a capital offence, but before he died Needs confessed to having committed murder at Messina in Italy. Then there was James Marsh, a Glastonbury man of 28 who was declared by the Chaplain, the Rev Theo. Rees, to be a hardened villain. He murdered a fellow servant Robert Parsons in 1816 but wouldn't say why. From all accounts he and Parsons had lived together on the best of terms and had never been heard even to quarrel. One day he knocked Parsons down, cut his throat and threw the body in a ditch. He was hanged on 8 April 1816.

Another example of a dispute between workmates was reported in the *Sherborne, Dorchester & Taunton Journal* in November 1838. Apparently William Stacey and James Osmond, employees of a Mr Axtens of Milborne Port, had been cutting clover all day when they began to argue (they'd also had a fair amount to drink). Stacey reproached Osmond for breaking his scythes and throwing them into a brook. Not realising Osmond was armed, Stacey accepted a challenge to fight and stripped to the waist. Osmond eventually stabbed him with a knife, gashing him in the belly until his bowel spilled out.

A witness ran to fetch the local surgeon, William Best, who spent 20 minutes performing an on-the-spot operation. Then the two men helped Stacey home; en route the wound reopened and soon after they met another surgeon, named Barrett, who accompanied the party and performed a second operation. Despite the surgical assistance, Stacey died the next day (Mr Barrett reckoned there were fifteen stab wounds in all). Following the coroner's inquest, Osmond was arrested and taken to Ilchester Gaol, remaining there until April for his trial at the next Western Assizes. The knife was found in the field some 20 yards from the scene of the fight, and handed to Mr Axtens to produce in court as evidence. The jury returned a verdict of manslaughter against Osmond who was sentenced to 14 years transportation.

James Pearce, a native of Frome and 27 years old, was one perhaps who deserved clemency and didn't get it. He had shot James Hellard, the landlord, in the Rock public house near Taunton. Pearce's defence, right to the last, was that he didn't know the gun was loaded, although he did admit to bearing a grudge against Hellard. No one in court would believe believe him and he was hanged at Ilchester on 22 August 1814.

A colourful account of the affair appeared in the recently published *Crime and Punishment in Regency Frome: Journals of*

Isaac Gregory, Constable of Frome 1813–14, 1817–18. Gregory named the victim as James Kellard of the Rack Public House, and wrote that Pearce, who had been drinking at the bar from noon until 8pm, was about to leave when Kellard asked him to pay for 'two pots of cyder'. Pearce 'flew into a great passion. Said he did not owe anything, struck the Landlord several times. Landlord ordered him into the custody of witness.' Kellard/Hellard fetched some handcuffs, but couldn't get them on Pearce who again became violent. He threw off his clothes and then insisted on being handcuffed. 'Witness begged him to be peacable. He seemed quiet and witness fell asleep by his side being overcome by Liquer.' The witness (not named) was woken by the sound of a gun, saw Pearce had one in his hand and the landlord lying on the ground.

A second man who was employed by Hellard and had been out in the fields scaring birds with the gun testified that upon returning to the Rock he had put the loaded gun in its place behind the bar; it was not cocked. He had been sitting in the kitchen when Hellard had returned to the bar and the gun was fired. He ran into the bar as his master toppled forwards onto the floor. The journal continues: 'For the prisoner, a witness said at the inquest the gun had went off at half cock. The Judge and Jury tryed it at half cock. It would not go off, neither could witness make it go off at half cock' — perhaps it's as well, otherwise there might have been a second corpse.

Later in the trial the 'Judge (was) charged with being drinking sherry … upon which he was taken into custody a few minutes' (is this how judges behaved in Regency England?). 'Verdict Guilty. Death. Judge and Court was in tears at the solemnity of the Judge in passing sentance. Prisoner was very indifferent to his fate. Looks about unconcerned all the time. Was picking an orange and eating of it carelessly as if he didn't want it.' Following execution, Pearce's body was returned for burial to Frome at the Wesley Chapel; his friends were convinced the trial was unfair.

A seemingly senseless murder was carried out in 1818 by Mark Shepherd (or Sheppard, according to the Register of the Gaol), who murdered a shoemaker, William Cornish. Both men lived in the small village of Stoke St Michael, so presumably they knew each other. Until a few minutes before mounting the scaffold at Ilchester, Shepherd denied killing Cornish, but finally he admitted his guilt and said another person had assisted, but wouldn't say whom (the chaplain thought the brother was implicated). And so the record went on — every year a few hangings for murder, many more for sheep stealing, horse stealing, forging money, robbery with violence, the occasional rape and quite a number for acts of bestiality and 'unnatural acts'. Then, in 1842, there was a particularly bad outbreak of typhus and it was decided that the prison had become too antiquated to continue in use. Wilton Gaol in Taunton became the County Gaol and all prisoners were transferred from Ilchester. By September 1842, with the old gaol empty, a committee appointed to oversee the sale of the place ordered that advertisements be placed in various newspapers, including *The Times*.

A little house on the north bank of the river, west of the bridge, was often called the Hanging House, but it was not built until 1845 and was, in fact, used as a summerhouse by Henry Tuson whose family bought the gaol buildings. The bakehouse and the wash-house were converted to dwellings, but most of the buildings were demolished and the stone was used to build a row of houses in Almshouse Lane. A petrol station stands on part of the site, and Gallows Five Acres, where so many died before crowds of excited onlookers, isn't even marked on the Ordnance Survey 1:50 000 maps, although several sites of single executions within the county are still recorded.

2

Lady Agnes Hungerford:
Did She Do It, or Was She Framed?

S ome murders took place so long ago that it is impossible to know the true story. What, for instance, lay behind the trial of Agnes Hungerford for the murder of her first husband, John Cotell, in 1518? Was she guilty of causing his death? and if so, why did the law wait until the natural death of her second husband, Sir Edward Hungerford in 1522? A man, incidentally, who was obviously so happy with Agnes (who was his second wife) that he made her his sole heir to the exclusion of the son of his first marriage. Had Edward not made such a will, would Agnes have been left in peace?

At that time the property of a convicted felon was forfeit to the Crown, and among the State Papers of Henry VIII is an 'Inventory of the Goodes belongyng to the Kynges Grace by the forfettoure of the Lady Hungerford, atteynted of murder in Hillary Terme, Anno xiiij. Regis Henrici viij.' A long list of plate and jewellery, furniture and hangings and of clothing shows that Agnes was well provided for. Knowing how rapacious Henry could be, might his agents not have been on the lookout for those whose goods would be worth seizing by legal means? Also, what man would knowingly marry a murderess and then invite her to repeat the crime by making such a will? Might Sir Edward himself have been involved in the murder of John Cotell? We shall never know.

The Hungerfords were a fairly important family – the name is still commemorated today by London's Hungerford Bridge. One branch of the family lived at Farleigh Castle, in the village of Farleigh Hungerford in Somerset, and they're the ones this story describes. Edward was first married to Jane, daughter of John, Lord Zouche of Haryngworth (stained glass that showed their joint coat of arms was found during the late nineteenth century in a cottage at Wellow and is now in Farleigh Hungerford Church), and by her had a son in 1503. Edward served in the French wars in 1513 and was knighted at Tournai on 25 December 1513. His father, Sir Walter Hungerford, Kt, died in 1516 and Edward inherited his property, living, it is believed, for some of the time at Farleigh Hungerford. He attended Henry VIII at a banquet at Greenwich on 7 July, 1517, and on 7 November in the same year was appointed Sheriff for Wiltshire (he also had property at Heytesbury).

In 1520 he was nominated to attend the English sovereign at the Field of Cloth of Gold when the French and English kings met with the intention of forming an alliance. In February 1521 he was in the Commission of the Peace for Somerset. In the same year, on 14 December, he made his last will, describing himself 'of hole and perfite mynde and of good memory, being sike in body' and he asked to be buried in the parish church at Heytesbury. He died on 24 January, 1522, most likely at his house at Heytesbury. Altogether a worthy sounding gentleman.

His son, Lord Walter, on the other hand, was a thoroughly nasty piece of work who was beheaded for buggery in 1540 alongside Thomas Cromwell, Earl of Essex, who was executed for high treason. In the meantime, five months after Agnes's execution and following the seizure of her goods, Walter obtained a licence from the King to take over all his father's property (did he have a hand in accusing Lady Agnes?). He was a cruel husband to his three wives; two died, the third, having been locked up and treated appallingly, smuggled a letter to the monarch appealing for help.

But to go back to the story of Agnes Hungerford. There is no known documentary evidence as to what John Cotell did, nor how old he was, how old Agnes was, whether there were any children of their marriage, for how long they were mar-

The murder of John Cotell at Farleigh Castle

ried before the assassination, nor indeed from which family she came. Some goods forfeited to the King seemed to have belonged to Agnes before her second marriage, suggesting that John Cotell was not a poor man — possibly he was a steward or bailiff in the employ of Sir Edward Hungerford. We do know that he hailed from Heytesbury, the village where Sir Edward had property.

Whatever Cotell's profession, there was probably a legitimate reason for his being at Farleigh Castle, for it was there that he is alleged to have been throttled, suffocated and strangled with a kerchief by two men, William Mathewe (Maghewe, on a contemporary document) and William Inges. They then stuffed the body into the furnace of the kitchen and endeavoured to cremate it.

By December of 1518 Agnes was living at Farleigh Castle. From what little evidence that remains of the murder, the two murderers also lived at the castle (Agnes was later accused of harbouring them, but it is just as possible that Sir Edward allowed them to stay there and that he had connived in the deed). Nothing more is known of the affair until four years later when records show that on 25 August 1522, 'at Ilchester before John Fitz James and his fellow justices of oyer and terminer for the county of Somerset, William Mathewe, late of Heytesbury in the county of Wilts, yeoman, William Inges, late of Heytesbury in the county aforesaid, yeoman, on the 26th July, in the 10th year of the now Lord the King, with force of and arms made an assault upon John Cotell, at Farley, in the county of Somerset, by the procurement and abetting of Agnes Hungerford, late of Heytesbury in the county of Wilts, widow, at that time the wife of the aforesaid John Cotell.' All pleaded Not Guilty, and the case was thought to be sufficiently serious to be tried in London, and so the three accused were brought to the bar at Westminster on 27 November, 1522, by Sir Thomas Lovell, Constable of the Tower of London. Despite the pleas of innocency, all three were found guilty by the jury and were sentenced to be hanged at Tyburn.

William Inges sought to avoid the sentence by claiming benefit of clergy – that is, that he was a clerk in Holy Orders and therefore exempt from the sentence of the court. The Attorney General stated that Inges had married a woman named Joan Mason at Little Cheverell in Wiltshire and therefore was a bigamist (this was at a time when clergymen even in minor orders were required to be celibate), and the sentence should be carried out. Inges denied the marriage and so the Bishop of Salisbury was asked to make enquiries. Six months later, Inges, having been shown to be married, was hanged.

Agnes vanished from the pages of history for many years. According to The Chronicle of the Grey Friars of London, referring to events of 1523, 'And this yere in feverelle the xxti day, the lady Alys Hungrford was led from the Tower unto Holborne and there put into a carte at the churchyard with one of her servantes and so carried unto Tyborne and there both hangyd and she burryed at the Grayfreeres in the netherend of the myddes of the church on the North syde.'

John Stow, author of *The Chronicles of England*, and writing in 1580 of a time at least two years before his birth, referred to 'Lady Alice Hungerford, a knight's wife, for murthering her husband was led from the tower of London' and this helped to give credence to the belief that she had killed a Hungerford. The Hungerford records, which date back to the thirteenth century with the founding of the Hungerford Chantry at Salisbury, are strangely lacking in mention of Sir Edward; they showed no mention of a second marriage for Sir Edward to either Lady Alys, or to Lady Agnes.

Unfortunately, as parish records were not required to be kept at the time (a measure making them obligatory was introduced in 1530), church registers are not available to show where or when the two married. Over the years, however, a legend grew up that Agnes was hanged for poisoning Sir Edward. By the nineteenth century when there was an upsurge of interest in local history, the legend had become firmly entrenched.

The nineteenth-century passion for historical research brought to light the 'Inventory of the Goods of Dame Agnes Hungerford' referred to earlier. In 1859 the Rev John Edward Jackson transcribed one of the documents from the time of Henry VIII, now preserved in the Public Record Office, and was able to shed some light on the story of Lady Agnes and Sir Edward, but even he had it wrong, and it was left to William John Hardy in 1880 to unravel the story – but even he had no doubt of Agnes's guilt. And we shall never know the full facts.

3
The Case of the Missing Curate

Most of what is known of this rather curious crime has been gleaned from four pages, torn from a pamphlet that was published in 1624, and 'printed by Edw: Allde for Natheniell Butter.' Entitled *The crying Murther*, it concerned the death of a Somerset curate, and yet it came to light in 1744 in a wooden chest in the church of East Harling in Norfolk.

The fragment describes 'the cruell and most horrible Butcher of Mr Trat, Curate of olde Cleave', which ended in the execution at Stone Gallows near Taunton of 'young Peter Smethwicke, Andrew Baker, Cyril Austen and Alice Walker' on 24 July 1624.

Apparently John Trat was an outspoken young gentleman who did not hesitate to use his pulpit to rebuke those of his parishioners he believed to be straying from the straight and narrow. It would seem from the pamphlet, that an 'honest woman' had been molested and Mr Trat hadn't shrunk from thundering forth on the enormity of the offence. Life for the black sheep among his parishioners was definitely an uncomfortable business, and matters probably came to a head when it was heard that the parish incumbent, one Rev Edward (or Edmund) Brigandine (Weaver's *Somerset Incumbents* gives the name as 'Brickenden'), had resolved to resign the living of Old Cleeve, and Mr Trat was thought to have bought it from him. This did not please young Peter Smethwicke, son (or more probably the grandson) of the patron, presumably because either he had hoped to take over the incumbency or, more likely, was one of the malefactors at whom the curate's wrath was directed.

For whatever reason, Peter Smethwicke, together with

Baker, Austen and Alice Walker, lay in wait for Mr Trat on the Wednesday after Midsummer's Day, 1624. They murdered him, 'with two mortal wounds in the chest', as he was returning along the road after taking some money and provisions to his mother. They hid the corpse and next day collected it and dragged it to the curate's own house.

And now comes the gruesome part of this story. The conspirators set to work and cut up the body. They disembowelled it and quartered it; they burnt the head and 'privy members', parboiled the flesh and then salted it to prevent it rotting and causing a smell. The arms, legs, thighs and bowels were 'powdred up into two earthen steenes or pots in a lower room of the house' and the rest of the carcase was placed in a vat.

According to one account, the father of young Peter Smethwicke next entered the story. In order 'to present an alibi', he dressed himself in some of Mr Trat's clothing and went to the house of John Ford, a Taunton bowmaker, saying that he was Trat. He spent two weeks in Taunton, impersonating the cleric, but to no avail. Parishioners in Old Cleeve became suspicious at the absence of zealous John Trat and began to search for him. Two weeks after the murder, his remains were discovered. How suspicion came to light on the four is not known. Possibly conscience intervened, and one confessed, possibly there was some boasting among comrades at having rid the parish of its turbulent priest, but somehow the word got around.

The conspirators were arrested and taken before Lord Chief Justice Baron Tanfield at the Somerset Assizes in Taunton. Justice was dispensed swiftly in those days – the end came for the four within five weeks of committing the crime.

The Stone Gallows no longer exists; a public house erected alongside the A38 commemorates the name, and although the sign shows a gallows made of stone, the name derives from a hamlet called Stone, next to the parish of Bishops Hull, just west of Taunton.

The crying Murther:

Contayning the cruell and most horrible Butcher
of Mr. T R A T, Curate of olde *Cleaue*; who was first murther
as he trauailed vpon the high way, then was brought home to his hou
and there was quartered and imboweld: his quarters and bowels being:
t. rwards perboyld and salted vp, in a most strange and feare full manner. For this fact
the Iudgement of my Lord chiefe Baron T A N F I E L D, young *Peter Smethwicks, A*
drew Baker, Cyrill Austen, and *Alice Walker*, were executed this last Summer
Assizes, the 2 ¼. of Iuly, at Stone Gallowes, neere Taunton
in Summerset-shire.

AT LONDON:
Printed by *Edw: Allde* for *Nathaniell Butter.*
1 6 2 4.

The frontispiece to 'The crying Murther', showing the remains of the
unfortunate John Trat being cut up.

The executions of Alice Walker and Messrs Smethwicke, Baker and Austen at Stone Gallows were the first recorded time that the site had been used, but it most definitely was not the last.

Newspapers of the day supplied details of a few crimes that were committed in the eighteenth century but, as communications were still poor and as the Stamp Duty, imposed in 1712, put such commodities outside the reach of most people, newspapers were few and far between and had to cram the entire nation's news into four pages.

More information was available from the Chaplain's Diary, compiled by the Rev Theo. G. Rees (and now deposited at the Somerset Record Office). This document covers the period 1789 to 1821 and lists the crimes and sentences of many prisoners who were held at Ilchester Gaol. Some entries were laconic, others recorded the chaplain's feelings concerning a particular prisoner. Some of the unfortunate inmates were hanged at the gaol, others died at various places around the county, including a surprising number who were taken to Stone Gallows to meet their end – and they are the ones that are described here.

On 21 April 1738, Nathaniel Wethyman was executed for the murder of his master, 'Farmer Trott'. Apparently, when Wethyman was sent to cut brambles and bind up the faggots, he decided instead to leave his work and go to have a drink at the Catherine Wheel at Ashill. He was having an affair with a maid who worked at the pub and, obviously, a dalliance and a pint were more appealing than clearing the hedge. Farmer Trott caught him in the pub and sent him back to his work. Later he spoke harshly to Wethyman about his affair. The rebuke so stung the labourer that he hit Trott smartly over the head with a stake and then, producing a knife, he stabbed him twice in the breast and left the knife in his throat. Presumably both master and murderer lived in the Hatch Beauchamp/Ashill area, but I could find nothing more about this case.

The inn sign showing the stone gallows.

Quite a number of those who died at Stone Gallows were executed for 'ordinary' murders: 29-year-old Joan Tottle killed her bastard child in 1793 and paid the penalty on 3 April; Thomas Withys, born at Pilton, was executed on 31 March 1794 for the murder of his wife – he was 24 years old. Then there was John Isaacs, alias Wilmot, aged 38, born at Whitelackington near Ilminster, died 2 April 1798 for the murder of John Wilmott (or Wilmot) at Bath. The *Western Flying Post* of 9 April 1798 noted that Isaacs had been 'a resident for these last fourteen years at Bath'. Wilmot, the victim, was a bailiff who had been collecting rent arrears of three and a half guineas. Isaacs 'seemed little affected at his awful situation even to the last' but along with the other two was noted by the chaplain in his diary as acknowledging his guilt.

Mr Rees had more to say about Thomas Gage, alias Torr or Tarr. 'A more hardened villain in so early life perhaps never was executed ... the night before he suffered he confessed to the murder and how he perpetrated it and likewise where he had secreted the things he had stolen from the house of the murdered person.' Despite a search, nothing was found of the stolen goods and the chaplain remarked that Gage's father was strongly suspected of taking them away. The diary noted that Gage, aged 18, was born at Kingsbrompton (now Brompton Regis) and was hanged at Stone Gallows, in what proved to be the last execution there, on 9 April 1810 for the murder of what reads like 'Eley Stylrig'. Examination of other records shows that he was committed by C.H.H. Tynte, charged on strong suspicion of the murder of his mistress Sarah Styling (elsewhere she is referred to as Elizabeth Styling) and of robbing the house.

Sarah, aged 27, had been married for four years, she had no children. She was sitting at tea when Gage hit her. Her husband had been helping a neighbour with his wheat sowing and came home to find his barn doors open and his wife dead in the kitchen. His mare had gone; Gage had absconded, taking two notes of £10 each, the mare, some silver coin, several silver spoons, a greatcoat and a gown. The mare was found on Brundon Hill and two days later Gage was found at his parents' home at Kingsbrompton. His name actually was Tarr. He'd run away from an apprenticeship at Kingsbrompton the previous midsummer.

Further information concerning the case came from material deposited at the Public Records Office in London. In the Jurors' Statement Sarah is surnamed Stillen, the wife of Henry Stillen. Gage, 'with a certain Hatchet made of Iron and wood of the value of one shilling' had in his right hand 'held her the said Sarah Stillen in and upon the right side of the

head near the right ear and upon the left side of the head
thereby giving her divers mortal wounds bruises and frac-
tures of which she instantly died.' The Back Calendar of
Taunton Assizes 31 March 1810 recorded the verdict:
'Thomas Gage otherwise called Thomas Tarr: Attainted of
Petit Treason. Let him be drawn on Monday the ninth day of
April next to the place of Execution and there Let him Be
Hanged by the Neck until he be dead and Let the Body be delivered to Mr John Buncombe a surgeon to be dissected and
anatomised pursuant to the Statute for preventing the horrid
crime of murder.'

The Gaol Bill for 1810 showed that 'The Sheriff of Somer-
setshire authorised To Wm Bridle, Keeper of his Gaol at Ivel-
chester, April 9 Thomas Gage alias Torr executed for Murder:
£2.00.' The worst part of the sentence in the eyes of people of
that time was the order for the body to be delivered for dissec-
tion – that was tantamount to condemning a man to eternal
damnation – no body, no resurrection, no life hereafter.

Thomas Gage may have been a hardened criminal in the
eyes of the Rev Mr Rees, but he (and another cleric) regarded
more kindly James Taylor, who also died at Stone Gallows.
Taylor, aged 23, was the only son of Grace Roy, by a former
husband. Mrs Roy kept a public house, The Bell, on Stall
Street in Bath. The lad had been taught to read and write but
had had little religious training and no sense at all of moral ob-
ligation. He associated with bad company and led a very dissolute life and was much indulged by his doting mother. He
also had a loving wife and a young child.

According to Taylor's own account, on 22 December 1808,
having had his tea he left his mother's house for a while.
When he returned he looked in at the tap room and saw a
stranger sitting by the fire together with a coachman named
Guion. Guion started to joke with Taylor about two women
who had quarrelled on his account. Taylor then went upstairs
to his bedroom to join the companion with whom he had

spent much of the day, but he wanted to learn more of what
had happened between the women, so he returned to the tap
room. There John Dyer, a particular friend, joined the party
along with David Rice, a nodding acquaintance who had a
woman in tow.

The evening was spent in gaming and drinking; Taylor said
he took no part in the former except to decide who was the
winner. A man called Johnson became abusive when Rice
was declared the winner, and Taylor and Johnson began to
fight. They went out of the room and down some of the cellar
steps where Johnson gave in and the two men shook hands.
Taylor found that, without realising it, he'd stripped off his
shirt, and Johnson discovered that he'd lost a brooch. Taylor
told him not to worry, he'd replace it, but Johnson said he
wanted the original because it had his name on it – so Taylor
said he'd go and search for it.

Just then, swearing that Johnson should have his brooch,
Guion snatched the candle from Taylor and found the pin at
the bottom of the cellar stairs. In his drunken state he
rounded on Taylor, whereupon those two began to fight, and
Guion called on Johnson for help. Johnson came; he didn't in-
terfere but just stood watching the fight. Guion grabbed
Taylor's shirt sleeves and he slipped out of the garment, but
when Guion called for a poker, Taylor ran upstairs to his bedroom closely followed by his mother.

Had he stayed there, things would probably have calmed
down. Mrs Roy tried to persuade him to stay in his room but
Taylor reported that he, being furious at Guion's behaviour,
snatched up two loaded pistols and ran downstairs again.
Rice and his female companion were at the bottom of the
stairs. Taylor tried to frighten them away, but upon hearing
his mother shriek 'Murder, murder', he rushed into the tap
room to see her lying on the settle supported by his (Taylor's)
wife and the maid servant. Guion, poker in hand, was standing before her. Taylor shot at Guion to prevent further injury

to Mrs Roy and then turned round and shot at the watchman, who had entered the pub upon hearing the shouting.

Taylor said he didn't know why he did it, but he began to beat the watchman; he came to his senses and went out into the street. When he returned the watchman was getting up off the floor. Taylor grabbed the poker from the maid's hand intending to strike again, but then he saw the blood running down the poor man's face. The watchman begged to be allowed to go free; Taylor told him to go and he replied that he couldn't as the door was shut. Just then the second watchman and a man named McGrath entered. Taylor surrendered himself to them, requesting that he should be taken safely to prison. Even then he didn't realise that he had shot his friend John Dyer in mistake for Guion.

While in prison Taylor was converted to Christianity. The Rev Thomas T. Biddulph of St James's, Bristol, frequently visited the young man and the two spent hours in prayer and contemplation of the scriptures. Taylor stood trial at the Taunton Assizes on 1 April. Later Biddulph reaped a more earthly reward when he published a small book entitled *Divine Mercy Exemplified in the case of James Taylor who was executed at Taunton on the Tenth of April 1809 for the murder of John Dyer*. It sold at one shilling a copy, and in 1813 was in its 3rd edition (printed and sold by Philip Rose, 20 Broadmead, sold also by F. & C. Rivington London and all other Booksellers). In it are reproduced Taylor's account of what happened and copies of letters written while at Ilchester and later at Taunton to his wife, his mother, brother and several friends, all telling of his new- found serenity and belief in Divine forgiveness.

It must have given great satisfaction to the chaplain.

4

Murder by Person or Persons Unknown

When you consider how the law was administered before Sir Robert Peel founded his Metropolitan police force in 1829, it is amazing how many crimes were solved. Apart from the Fielding brothers, Sir John and Henry (the latter of whom is better known as a novelist and author of *Tom Jones*), who were instrumental in setting up a training school for parish constables at Bow Street – the famous 'Bow Street runners', maintenance of law and order was a haphazard affair. The parish constable was a manorial post; the incumbent was chosen initially for one year but, if he proved satisfactory, he would remain in the position for several years. Even after the founding of the Metropolitan force this system continued for most of the country until 1856 with the passing of the County and Borough Police Act. Although many parish constables were reasonably honest and keen, others were corrupt. One advantage those early detectives had was that because poor roads discouraged travel and the vast majority of people tended to go no further than their own legs or a horse could take them, a good parish constable knew far more about the inhabitants of 'his' patch than any policeman does today. He had watched them grow up, he had an idea of who was most likely to commit what crime and the method which he (or she) would adopt.

Strangers to a district were noticed immediately and, with a lack of other entertainment, far greater interest in their activities was shown by neighbours. Knowledge of a motive (dishonesty towards others, cuckolding of husbands, aggressiveness towards certain individuals) led to suspects and few people were prepared to commit perjury and so endanger their immortal souls for eternity in order to provide a false alibi. Cases where a reward was offered were generally solved more expeditiously than those that carried no such incentive. There were, however, some murders for which no motive was apparent, and no witnesses. Such cases were usually the ones left with an open file by the coroner.

The murder of a Mr Stuckey is a typical example. He was a builder who on 9 August, 1830, left his home in Chard to go to Stratton, near South Petherton, on business. He called at Chillington on his return journey, leaving about 10pm, and was not seen alive again. There was an extensive search for him, but not until 30 August was his body found, in a field on the side of the lane leading from Chillington to Dinnington, some 200 to 300 yards from a lodge of the Hinton St George estate, home of the Poulett family.

The builder's head had been nearly severed from his body. In his pockets were his watch, his pocket book and slide rule – all items of value to a thief. Four shillings and six pence were also found in his trouser pockets and other coins were scattered nearby. There seemed to be no motive for his death whatever. He was a good employer and no one was known to have a grudge against him.

Eventually a Bow Street runner was sent to investigate the case. Despite the fact that a £500 reward was offered (to be raised, incidentally, by public subscription), no one came forward with evidence and so there was never a need to try to raise the money for the reward.

No one person was found to be responsible for the murder of Lieutenant Compton Eure in 1640, but the authorities were able to write 'finis' in that particular case in a rather unfair manner.

Lt Eure was with a troop of infantry who halted in Wellington en route from Devon. It was a Sunday, and the young officer, presumably being very tired, failed to attend church. His men were devout Protestants and some decided that his absence from church was an indication that he was a Papist. They took him to the church porch, pushed him to the ground, tied him behind a horse and dragged him around the town. Then they barbarously murdered him. Meanwhile others of the troop, obviously believing in guilt by association, demolished the house where he had been staying. The troop then immediately disbanded, all going their separate ways. Letters went to and from London and Charles I's State Papers show that orders were given to cut off funds for the troop, but none of those guilty could be traced. So the blame was put on the folk of Wellington and a £200 fine was levied on the town for allowing the miscreants to escape.

More than a century and a half later a murder occurred where the authorities were almost sure they had arrested the perpetrators. In 1808, a drummer named Pat Chasty was found dead, floating in the River Tone at Taunton. Four men were arrested, tried and acquitted. No one else was accused of the crime and no further investigations were made. A local druggist named Farmery managed to get hold of Pat Chasty's skull and he displayed it in his shop to advertise his wares. Years went by, two of the acquitted men died, but then in 1832 interest in Pat Chasty was rekindled when, as a result of drunken confidences in the Black Boy public house (later re-named the Princess Royal), the two survivors were arrested again, tried once more for the same crime (presumably the charge was worded differently, since no one can be tried twice on the same charge following an acquittal), and once more acquitted. The one incident of note in that particular trial was the fact that the Assize judges complained of there being a shortage of beer provided for them in their lodgings!

A most foul and mindless slaughter took place in 1773 at a hamlet a mile north of Monksilver. An 88-year-old widow, Mrs Elizabeth Conibeer, lived with her two unmarried daughters, Anne aged 45 and Sarah, 43, at Woodford. They had few visitors, but one who did come regularly to their little cottage was a baker's lad. He was expected on 5 June, there was a pile of pennies on the table and the three women were eating their midday meal. Outside it was a brilliantly sunny day. Then someone struck, slashing out at all three women with a sharp instrument. Blood was splashed all over the place – the lad was probably only a short distance off when the slaughter took place, yet he heard nothing. He entered the open door, saw the gory scene and turned and fled for help; his prompt retreat saved his life, for the murderer was almost surely still at the scene of the crime. No one ever was suspected or charged with the deed, and the three victims lie in the churchyard at Monksilver in one grave.

A mass murder that took place many centuries ago was only discovered in 1970. Archaeologists were excavating the site of Cadbury Castle when they came across the bones of some thirty men, women and children. The skeletons were in various stages of dismemberment; some had no skulls, others had lost one or more limbs, and the sight was so gruesome to some of the volunteer 'diggers' that they refused to work on the site. There is no way of knowing exactly what did take place, but from the evidence historians have concluded that the massacre took place some time in the first century AD, well after Boudicca's uprising. The Romans were keen to remove the native peoples from their hill forts and resettle them in newly founded lowland towns. In the case of Cadbury Castle it was obvious that the inhabitants had been forewarned. They had reinforced the barricades and increased the height of the soil around the ramparts of their settlement. Their efforts were useless against the greater might of the Roman army with its more sophisticated weaponry, and those defending the south west gate were slaughtered where they stood. The remainder of the inhabitants were rounded up and taken off to their new homes in Ilchester and Catsgore, leaving the bodies of the dead where they fell.

Wild animals, including wolves, which were still prevalent

Wellington Monument, scene of the death of Bessie Wilton in 1917.

in Britain during those times, pulled the remains to pieces. Later the Roman army returned to finish the task of demolishing the fort. The timbers around the gate were burnt and the ashes and charred remains helped to cover the heap of bodies. Whether one regarded the massacre of those people as murder or not at the time depended upon whether one was Roman or Briton, but certainly there'd have been no coroner's inquest on those poor souls and no one would have worried about who was responsible for their demise.

Sometimes a rumour starts at the death of a person and, no matter what is said, local hearsay insists that there was 'dirty work at the crossroads'. Such was the case of Mrs Bessie Wilton. During my search for stories of murders, time and time again I was told, 'You must include the story of the housekeeper who was found murdered at the foot of Wellington's Monument'.

According to these reports, the police found bloodstains all the way down the steps inside the monument, consistent with a body falling and bumping against the walls. They carried out a series of experiments to duplicate the falling, but the dummy came to rest partway down. One informant told me that the lady worked for a local shopkeeper and that both of them had left his house after lunch one early closing afternoon. He had then taken her up to the monument and at the top had killed her, dragging her body to the bottom of the tower and there leaving it to be discovered.

Such a story sounded as though it would make the headlines of *The Times* – but a search of the index proved fruitless; a search of the Assize Records for Somerset turned up no mention of a trial, and yet all my informants seemed positive that the employer, Charles Scott Hammett, did the evil deed, some going so far as to say he stood trial and was acquitted for lack of evidence. I am indebted to Gillian Allen, Wellington's local historian, who by dint of reading through each issue of the *Wellington Weekly News* from its foundation in 1870 tracked down the true story.

Mrs Bessie Wilton was a widow aged 47. Wellington's Monument, a tall slender column erected by the people of Wellington in honour of the Iron Duke, stands atop a ridge of the Blackdown Hills overlooking the town. The monument held a strange fascination for Mrs Wilton, and one morning in 1917 she left her employer's house very early and made her way there. One mystery that never was solved was how she got inside the column, because the entry to the inside staircase was locked each evening at sunset and not unlocked again until a respectable hour in the morning. But get inside the column she did and, furthermore, she climbed to the top.

Mrs Wilton was very short sighted and at the inquest the coroner decided she had stepped back at the top of the 175-ft tower, toppled backwards down the stairs, and had continued falling, because with each attempt to save herself she started the momentum again. He was of the opinion that she was still alive when she reached the bottom and had tried to get outside for some fresh air. It was only then that she collapsed and died, and that would explain why, when found, her forehead was resting on her fist, as though she had been trying to go back up the column. Her shoes were found separately on the stairs, and she had bled from wounds as she hit the stonework.

Mr Scott Hammett, a bachelor with a reputation above reproach, was still fast asleep in bed when Mrs Wilton left to keep her appointment with death, but in this particular instance the murder committed by person or persons unknown was to his reputation, and sadly it persists to this day.

5
The Hartgill Murders

The venue of this story, Kilmington, became part of Wiltshire on September 30 1896, but in 1556 it was considered
to be in Somerset. At one time it was the property of the
Crown, but later passed to the Hartgills. While Edward VI
was on the throne William Hartgill was appointed a Commissioner for the Survey of Churches and Chapels, and presumably was a member of the Church of England. He is also said to
have been Steward to William, 7th Baron Stourton.

Charles, 8th Baron Stourton of Stourton, was typical of the
worst of the aristocracy. Rude and argumentative with his
peers, appallingly oppressive and tyrannical to those who
were below him in rank, he assembled a gang of thugs around
him and terrorised the neighbourhood. He first crossed
swords with the Hartgills when he illegally enclosed some
common land and they sought a royal mandate that put an
end to the enclosures. It has also been suggested that Charles
Stourton was an adherent to the Roman Catholic faith (hence
his later appeal to Queen Mary) and this difference in religious persuasion fanned his hatred of the Hartgill family.

One account states that soon after the death of William, 7th
Baron Stourton in September 1548, his widow, Dame
Elizabeth took up residence at Kilmington, and that Charles
went to the house to try to persuade his mother to enter into a
bond involving a large amount of money conditional upon
her promising never to remarry. He asked Hartgill to influence her, which he only agreed to do provided Stourton made
generous provision for her from his vast fortune. Another account states that Hartgill took the part of William's mistress,
Agnes Ryse, when she claimed the bedding and plate left to

her in Baron Stourton's will. Charles then accused William
Hartgill of possessing himself of property rightly belonging
to the Stourtons. Hartgill complained to the Council at
Whitehall and as a result Charles Stourton was committed to
the Fleet Prison in 1550. He was not the kind of man to forget
such actions.

On Whit Sunday morning in 1555 (or 1556, authorities dis-
agree on the dates) Stourton visited Kilmington taking with
him a group of retainers, all of whom were armed with
crossbows and arrows or with guns. He complained that the
Hartgill father and son had been hunting with dogs and
horses in his park.

William Hartgill and his wife, along with a few of their servants took refuge in the church belfry and were kept prisoner
there by Stourton and his gang. Young John Hartgill rode to
London to report to Sir Thomas Speke, the High Sheriff of
Somerset, what had happened, and on the following Wednesday the Sheriff arrived at Kilmington Church and had the
Hartgills and their party released. While imprisoned in the
tower William had had to watch his favourite mount being
shot with a crossbow by one of Stourton's men because, it
was claimed, it had been ridden by Hartgill while hunting in
his lord's park.

Stourton was soon back in the Fleet Prison. He wasn't there
long (his father married a half-sister of the Duke of Northum-
berland and ducal influence where his nephew was concerned soon effected a release). He was called before the
Council and promised faithfully to behave, declaring that if
cattle or horses from the Hartgill estates strayed onto his land,
the Hartgills would be free to come and fetch them. Some animals did stray and while William and John were en route to
collect the animals some dozen of Stourton's thugs set upon
them and John was left for dead on the road. The Court of Star
Chamber fined Stourton an amount to be paid over to his victims and again committed him to the Fleet Prison. On his re-

lease he determined that the father and son should never again give him trouble.

There was some discussion as to whether the money Stourton owed the Hartgills should be paid over in the church, in the church house, or across a table set on the open green in front of the church. The Hartgills met Stourton at Kilmington Church on 11 January 1556/7 for the settlement, but they soon realised there was trouble ahead. In front of a conclave of some sixty persons, justices, gentlemen, tenants and approximately sixteen of Stourton's retainers, Stourton arrested William Hartgill, charging him with felony and, together with his son John, thrust him violently into the church house and had both men tightly bound. Stourton himself took charge of the Hartgills' purses and later gave a turquoise he found in one to Lady Stourton.

John Hartgill's wife rushed to the church house and was first kicked by Stourton and then struck on the neck by him with his sword 'and for three hours the company had much ado to keep life in her'.

The Hartgills were taken to the Parsonage at Kilmington and later to Bonham, a house owned by Stourton. There they were kept bound for a day and a night without heat, food or water and with nothing to lie on. On the afternoon of the second day they were taken to a 'close' near Stourton and forced to kneel with their hands tied behind them. Clubbed on the head, they still lived, so Charles Stourton ordered that their throats should be cut with a knife 'my Lord standing by with the candle in his hand'. The bodies were tumbled into a dungeon and were buried under a deep covering of earth, then with 'two courses of thick paving' and finally with two cartloads of shavings and chips of timber that were spread over the grave.

Sir Anthony Hungerford later exhumed the bodies and Charles, Lord Stourton, was arrested on 28 January and taken to the Tower of London. He was arraigned at Westminster

Hall on 26 February and found guilty and sentenced to hang. Four of his minions were also arrested and they probably were executed in London.

Charles Stourton petitioned Queen Mary for some indulgence, but all she would allow was that he should be hanged with a silken rope. He was executed in the Market Place at Salisbury on 6 March 1556/7 and that silken rope was placed over his tomb in Salisbury Cathedral where it remained for many years.

6

The Story of Poor John Walford

D uring the eighteenth century there lived at Over
Stowey a family named Walford. The husband was described as a collier, a maker of charcoal from wood, and he
also kept horses for carrying the charcoal. His son John, who
was born in 1765, was reported by some who knew him to
have been a good tempered and generous young man who
could neither read nor write; other reports made him out to be
surly and morose – but that was after he had been arrested for
murder.

Young John Walford fell in love with Ann Rice, the daughter of a miller. Although she had been well educated and was
clever, she loved him dearly and they planned to marry. Accordingly she went to live for a while with John's family. His
mother had died and the father had remarried a spiteful, vindictive woman who somehow persuaded the young couple
to postpone their marriage.

John was also a charcoal maker. He spent the working
week in the woods, returning home each Saturday night and
appearing next morning at church neatly dressed and well
scrubbed. During his week-long sojourn in the woods he saw
very few people, but one young girl from the village, ostensi-
bly out collecting wood for the fire, used to seek out John. She
was not very bright, but rather crafty and somewhat slovenly.
Eventually she gave birth to a child and named John as the
father. According to the account of the affair contained in *The
Quantocks and their Associations*, by William Luke Nichols
(published in 1891 by Sampson Low), the parish officers took
John into custody and told him he must either marry the girl
or pay to support the child. A contemporary report of 1789

stated that it was not until Jenny (also called Jane in other accounts) became pregnant by John Walford a second time that the parish officers forced him to marry her.

The marriage took place on 18 June, 1789, and John took work as an husbandman, going home nightly to his semi-detached cottage in the village of Bincombe. For a few weeks the marriage appeared to have been tranquil. Jenny Walford formed the habit of visiting neighbours and spending hours talking with them. According to a story repeated to William Wordsworth, who lived at nearby Alfoxden from 1798–99, John intended to leave England and the wife he felt had trapped him into marriage, but his love for Somerset was so great he kept delaying his departure.

On July 5, a Saturday, he returned to his cottage after work and found his wife away from home. He called in on his next-door neighbours and had supper with them. After spending a couple of hours with them he went home to await his wife's return. That evening they were seen to be sitting peacefully together in the moonlight, then the door was shut and the couple seemed to have gone to bed.

At 12.30 that night, two young sisters who lived in the next-door cottage (whether it was the cottage where John Walford had supped, or the one on the other side of his home was not stated in the report) were waiting up for a third sister when they heard footsteps, as though of a bare-footed person, passing under their window. They looked out and saw John returning home.

It transpired that he had suggested to his wife that she should go to the Castle of Comfort at Dodington to have a drink of cider, and from his weekly wage of six shillings had given her one shilling (5p). She didn't want to go alone, so eventually he agreed to accompany her. According to his account, on the way to Dodington Jenny started an argument with him and he, maddened by the thought of his lost happiness, struck out at her and then realised that he had killed her.

He tried to drag her body to the mouth of a disused mineshaft, not far from Dodington churchyard. She was heavy and hard to move, so finally he abandoned her in a ditch, simultaneously retrieving his shilling. On the Sunday morning, between 6am and 7am, Jenny Walford's body was discovered at the place (according to some) now known as Dead Woman's Ditch.

John later confessed to the murder and declared it was un-premeditated. He was tried at Bridgwater on 18 August and found guilty by the Grand Jury. Despite the obviously sympathetic attitude of the judge, Lord Kenyon, the jury seemed bent on extracting the last little drop of blood from their pound of flesh. They asked that John should be hanged near the spot where he murdered his wife and then his body should be placed in irons and left there.

On his way to his execution on 20 August, John Walford asked whether Ann Rice might be brought to see him and they spent a final ten minutes together at the place where Jenny Walford's body had been found. Then, a contemporary report states, he joined in saying the Lord's Prayer and the Apostles' Creed and told the assembled crowd of some 3,000 spectators that he was guilty of the crime for which he was about to die but that he did it 'without foreintending it, and I hope God and the world have forgiven me.'

John was led about a quarter of a mile up the hill and hanged on a temporary gallows (watched by the crowd – a public hanging was regarded as an excuse for a holiday until the middle part of the nineteenth century). After some twenty minutes his body was taken down, placed in irons and drawn up about 30 feet on a gibbet erected for the purpose and there it stayed for some 18 months.

The site is marked even today on the Ordnance Survey 1:500 000 maps. The gibbet faced towards the front door of John's stepmother's home – possibly the sight of his decaying body gave her cause to regret her interference in the marriage

plans of Ann and John. A less gruesome memento of the
event was the erection of a fountain for the use of cottagers
living upon Dodington Common and for travellers to the
area.

*The fountain erected near Dodington as a memorial to Jenny Walford,
murdered by her husband in 1789.*

7
The Sad Story of Jane Buttersworth

Hemington, not far from Radstock on the east side of Somerset, was the scene of a particularly vicious and brutal murder in 1740. The victim was a girl of about 12 years old called Jane Buttersworth, who was beaten to death by the two women who employed her. Almost nothing is known of Jane's earlier life; apparently an orphan, she had been brought into the service of Mrs Elizabeth Branch and her daughter, Betty, by a John Lawrence, of Bristol. He told the child that she was bound apprentice and must therefore do all that she was told to do and must accept whatever was done to her.

A little more is known of Elizabeth Branch; she was the daughter of a one-time surgeon turned ship's master and had married a man named Benjamin Branch. The marriage was not happy and local gossip attributed Benjamin's death to poison administered by his wife. Elizabeth and daughter Betty seem to have been left in fairly comfortable circumstances (she had an income of £200 a year – a not inconsiderable sum when a farm labourer earned about £25 annually and servants could be obtained for £4 a year). They lived in Dover Castle, a house on a hill above Hemington. The property was large enough to warrant the employment of another female servant, Ann James; two men, William Budd and Henry Butler were also mentioned in court evidence as having worked there.

Jane's work was the most menial. It was she who scoured the pans, fed the calves, swept and scrubbed, and ran errands for her mistresses. Ann James reported that Jane was a civil girl who strove to obey the two women.

On 12 February, 1740 at about 8pm, Jane was sent the half
mile to the village of Faulkland to fetch bran from Anthony
Budd. She returned saying there was no bran. Next morning,
when William Budd, Anthony's son, reported for work, Mrs
Branch asked why no bran had been given to Jane and he
answered that no one came for it. Jane insisted that she had
gone to Faulkland and had been told there was none. Mrs
Branch first sent Ann into the garden to gather some withy
twigs from a tree growing near the house and then de-
spatched her to Faulkland to collect the bran.

Margaret Budd, wife of Anthony, confirmed that Jane had
not been there the previous evening. When Ann returned
from Faulkland she found Jane in the sheep house suckling
the calves and noticed that a wound on her arm was bleeding.
Betty Branch then came onto the scene. She asked Ann
whether Jane had been to Faulkland the previous evening
and upon being told 'no', started to beat the child. From the
sheep house they went into the kitchen where Mrs Branch
also took a rod made of withies and joined in the beating. The
mother told Ann to lay Jane on the floor and when she refused, saying it was better to send the girl away than to beat
her so, the two Branch women pushed Jane face down onto
the floor. Betty knelt on Jane's neck to hold her down and
both women whipped her until blood was running from the
various wounds. Then Betty took off one of Jane's shoes and
hit her with the heel while Elizabeth continued with the
whipping.

Ann asked the women to leave Jane alone and was told it
was none of her business. Betty kicked Jane and each woman
took up a stick again and hit her about the head and shoul-
ders. Jane tried to escape via the hall, but was hit back into the
kitchen. So much blood had been shed that Mrs Branch sent
Ann for a bucket of water and told Jane to wash it off herself.
The child was too weak, so Ann was told to clean her up, but
the blood was flowing too fast.

Jane Buttersworth.

Of the two women, Betty seems to have been the more vindictive. She ordered Jane to go into the courtyard beyond the kitchen to scour a kettle (saucepan?), but although she tried, Jane was just too weak. So then Ann was instructed by the women to set Jane to cleaning the hall and parlour with a brush. By then Jane was dizzy from loss of blood. Ann told the women Jane was sweeping the room but seemed in an odd way. Mrs Branch said unless Jane did better she'd be beaten again. The child was near fainting and Ann was sent to take her back to the kitchen. As they reached the steps leading to the courtyard Jane reeled, so they went outside for some fresh air. According to Ann's evidence, Betty Branch said to Jane: 'I will cool thee; you was too hot just now', and threw a half bucket of cold water over the girl's head and neck. Then she told Jane to dust out the room above the brewhouse across from the kitchen. Jane asked Ann to help her up the stairs.

Ann reported to the Branches that the child was too weak to do the work, whereupon Mrs Branch went upstairs and beat her again. Then she instructed Ann to send Jane to Faulkland for some hops, but realising that the girl was in no state to carry out the errand, the order was countermanded, and she was told to wash dishes in the brewhouse. Ann sat Jane beside the fire to carry out the task. In came Betty Branch carrying a pail of water; she sent Ann to fetch some salt. With the salt in her hand, Betty told Jane if she didn't soon wash the dishes, she would salt her breech (backside). The weakened child could do nothing, and so, in the presence of her mother, Betty Branch proceeded to rub salt into the bloody wounds. Ann was sent away on another task.

When she returned, Ann found Jane stretched on the floor. On her head was a clean cap that had become bloodstained. The girl did not answer when spoken to, and Ann presumed that she was dead. About 6pm the Branch women put Jane to bed and sent Ann to Faulkland for some wine. Upon her return two hours later, Ann went to the room she shared with Jane and reported to her employers that the child was dead. She was called a 'Welsh bitch' and told she'd only said Jane was dead to avoid having to sleep beside her. Ann stayed in her room from about 11 at night until 5 the next morning, Thursday, 14 February.

The women sent Ann that morning to fetch William Budd to make a coffin for Jane, and they warned her not to allow him to see the state of the body, but he later reported that he had seen one leg and one arm and both were black and badly bruised. Next day after dinner, Mrs Branch instructed Ann to warm some lye to wash the corpse because there were so many bruises that shouldn't be seen. Ann noticed even more wounds, including blood on the cap covering Jane's head.

John Lawrence, the man who had originally taken Jane to the Branch household, returned to the story on 18 February. He helped the two women put the body into the coffin. Mrs Branch pulled the bloodstained outer clothing off and then Ann had to cut the shift and its sleeves from the corpse under cover of a shroud. A shroud cap was pulled down low over the head and a black string was tied over the forehead to hide the bruising. Miss Branch locked Jane's clothing up in the apple store. The child was buried that evening.

Rumours, of course, were rife in the village. William Budd had asked Francis Coombes of Hemington to toll the bell on Friday the 15th, although it was customary for the passing bell to be sounded on the day of death or the morning immediately following. Mrs Branch made enquiries as to how deep the coffin had been buried and, when told it was about a yard down, replied that that was not deep enough. Villagers reported strange happenings in the churchyard – groaning sounds were heard, lights, like rockets, were said to be seen emanating from the grave of Jane Buttersworth.

Robert Carver and John Marchant, both of Hemington, were disturbed by these reports and, even more, by the rumours of murder. They decided to take action and, on the pretext of ringing the bells for Ash Wednesday 20 February, they obtained the key of the church. With several others they disinterred the coffin and took it into the church. Then they sent for the women who usually laid out the village dead (Mary Vigor and Betty Marchant were named in the evidence, but several others were sent for as well). The men reasoned that if nothing amiss were found with the body, they would quietly re-bury the coffin and then set about quelling the rumours.

Mary Vigor and Betty Marchant confirmed that, indeed, the body was greatly bruised and wounded. Messrs Carver and Marchant replaced the coffin lid, locked the church and took the key for safe keeping to the church warden, John Craddock. Next day, Thursday 21st, the constable and other parishioners arrested Elizabeth and Betty Branch.

The trial took place before the Hon Mr Justice Chapple at the Somerset Assizes on 31 March, 1740. Mrs Branch arrived well supplied with a large sum of money with which to bribe the jury. As a result there was a suggestion that the Sheriff should be the one to appoint the jury, but this was denied. After several challenges, the jury was sworn and the trial proceeded.

Mrs Branch was asked who laid out the corpse and she answered that she had; then she was asked why she hadn't sent for the usual women to carry out the task, no reply was recorded. Questioned as to whether she had seen any wounds on the body, she replied 'no'.

A Dr Salmon gave evidence. He testified to having examined the body twice and having found it badly injured, including broken skull bones. From the state of the wounds he thought she'd been beaten after she'd lost a great deal of blood.

Another witness, William Palmer, said that Mrs Branch had originally sent for his father-in-law, Mr Harris, a surgeon and apothecary of Bradford, to inspect the body on her behalf, but he, Mr Palmer, had been sent instead. Mrs Branch admitted that she and her daughter had beaten Jane Buttersworth but said that the girl must have damaged her head on a pail and that the neighbours must have wounded it further when they disinterred the body. Mr Palmer warned Mrs Branch that if he examined the body he'd be obliged to speak the truth as to when the wounds were inflicted, so she gave him a guinea for his pains and dismissed him. Mrs Branch is reported as having cross-examined him and asking him whether he knew that wilful murder had been returned by the coroner's inquest and Palmer replied yes.

William Coombes went with the constable and Ann James to search for the clothing that had been locked up in the apple chamber. Joined by several other searchers they could find no bloodied clothing; in fact the only item of Jane's apparel that they found was the skirt of her Sunday gown. Mr Coombes, however, saw some blood stains by the clock case in the kitchen, and against the brewhouse door, and more on the parlour floor. Ann James found two sticks which she removed from the house; these were later produced as evidence in court. One was a broomstick, the other was an ash stick, described as being above an ell (almost four feet) in length and tapering; on the large end was a blood mark. Ann James testified that both sticks were used on Jane.

In court Henry Butler stated that he had worked for the Branches and had frequently seen them beat Jane; he added that he, too, had also been beaten barbarously. Samuel Webber of Faulkland and William Budd of Hemington (son of the suppliers – or, rather, non-suppliers of the bran that started the whole sordid affair) both confirmed that they had heard Jane crying and Elizabeth Branch shouting on the fateful Wednesday.

The Branches fought back. Betty Branch said that the evidence was all malicious lies – the child had been destitute and she and her mother had fed and clothed her. John Lawrence, called in the Branches' defence, declared that Ann James was the perpetrator of all the wounds. And he'd heard Jane say that Ann used her badly. He also said that he'd put Jane into her coffin and that her shroud was put on in the usual way. Furthermore, he was with the Branches when the constable and parishioners came to the house and they could have escaped if they wished. Three witnesses, Francis Hales, John Craddock and Robert Carver, later gave a sworn statement that John Lawrence was already in custody when the constable and parishioners went to fetch the Branch women, and so they had no prior knowledge of the impending arrest. Another witness, Thomas Wrentmore, said he'd seen Ann James take Jane by the hair and hit her with a closed fist. According to Anne Paradise, she'd often heard Jane complain of hard usage from Ann, but never from the Branches.

Despite the testimony of witnesses in their defence, the two women were found guilty. Betty Branch complained that if the jury as first constituted had tried them, neither she and her mother would have been convicted. Later evidence showed that Jane did go to Faulkland for the bran, but because she had not been given money to pay for it, Margaret Budd refused to let Mrs Branch have credit. Presumably it was through fear of Elizabeth Branch's temper that Mrs Budd had lied when asked by Ann James whether the child had in fact gone to Faulkland on 12 February.

The Assize Records note that Elizabeth Branch and Betty Branch were both sentenced to death for the murder of Jane Battersworth, alias Buttersworth. Gaol Records show that these two unsavoury creatures were held at the Castle of Taunton. Their execution took place on 3 May 1740 at Ilchester. So great was the anger of people against the women that, fearing they might be lynched, the Governor ordered they should be hanged at 4am, much to the disappointment of the thousands who turned up several hours later to witness the hanging.

Another child murder was that of Betty Trump, whose story is partly recorded on a stone with the inscription 'Near this place Betty Trump was violated and murdered, February 20, 1823, aged 13 years. Thou shalt do no murder.' The stone was originally erected close to an old gravel pit at Coppice Burrows between Combe St Nicholas and Buckland. People began to avoid travelling along the nearby road at night be-

Betty Trump's headstone, Buckland St Mary.

cause a legend arose that the area was haunted by the ghost of
the dead girl and eventually the local authority deemed it best
to remove the stone and was said to have placed it in the
church at Buckland St Mary but, if so, a later authority moved
it elsewhere. Now all that remains is a grave near the south
side of the churchyard. The headstone, decorated with an or-
nate cross, leans at an angle, and the inscription is illegible,
but it is still possible to trace the word 'Sacred', and below it
'Betty Trump'.

Betty Trump was last seen alive in the shop of William Trea-
sure whose premises were on Holyrood Street in Chard. She
had made a few purchases and then begun the walk back to
her home at Buckland St Mary, a distance of some four miles.
On the way she was intercepted and it was presumed that,
because she resisted the attack by her violator, her throat was

cut. Her body was not found for three days. Three vagrants dressed as sailors were suspected at first, but no conclusive evidence that they had been in the vicinity of the gravel pit could be found. A reward of £50, then a considerable sum of money, was offered for evidence leading to the conviction of the killer, but was never claimed.

Suspicion fell on William Flood, a 26-year-old labourer in the employ of a local farmer Samuel Wyatt. Flood was a strange man; he had been brought up by Wyatt and had been decently educated and as a result was appointed to teach children in the Sunday School in which Betty Trump was a pupil. He admitted to having been in the vicinity of Coppice Burrows on the day that Betty disappeared and said that he had heard screams, but had assumed that they came from a nearby cottage. He had no explanation as to why he was unusually late back to his master's house on the day of the murder, nor did he see fit to mention to his master that he had heard screams. Flood was apprehended but soon released.

Then a Bow Street runner, appropriately named Samuel Hercules Taunton, was assigned to the case and again Flood was taken into custody, but this time he was committed to Ilchester Gaol on 8 April 1823 and tried in the Western Circuit Summer Assize at Bridgwater on 2 August. The court record shows that on the first count...' on the 20th day of February in the 4th year of our Sovereign Lord King George the Fourth, said William Flood with a certain knife of the value of six pence which he the said William Flood in his right hand then and there held the said Betty Trump in and upon the Neck and Throat of her the said Betty Trump then and there feloniously wilfully and of his malice aforethought did strike cut stab and penetrate giving the said Betty Trump then and there with the knife aforesaid in and upon the Neck and the Throat of the said Betty Trump one mortal wound of the length of ten Inches and the depth of five Inches. Of which mortal wound the said Betty Trump then and there instantly died.'

Possibly a conviction would have been obtained had there been only one count against Flood, but a second one charged further that '... the said William Flood not having the fear of God before his eyes but being moved and seduced as aforesaid...'(by the instigation of the Devil) '...did with a certain pocket handkerchief to the value of six pence... with both his hands put fasten and bind the said Handkerchief about the neck of Betty Trump... did choak (sic) and strangle of which choaking and strangling... she the said Betty Trump then and there instantly died.'

Mr Cox of Honiton defended Flood and despite the evidence of 45 witnesses, including John Wheadon, surgeon, Robert Uphill, the Coroner, and Joseph Salisbury, constable, the Judge expressed a doubt about there being sufficient evidence to warrant a conviction and the Grand Jury threw the case out. Incidentally, it would be interesting to discover whether the witness Martha Manning (of whose evidence there is no record in the Assize Records) was in any way related to the Wiveliscombe-born murderer, Frederick George Manning, whose story is told elsewhere in this book.

Suspicion never fell on any one else and throughout his life William Flood, who had become the tollgate keeper on the Honiton road, was shunned by the majority of those who knew of Betty's murder. William Flood on his deathbed was reported to have wanted to make a confession but his wife, who was standing beside him, closed his mouth with her hand saying, 'You have kept the secret all these years, you shall not let it out now.'

A third child murder was that of Emma Jane Davey of Yeabridge, South Petherton, murdered in January 1889 at the time Jack the Ripper was terrorising the East End of London and providing wonderful copy for imaginative news reporters. Somehow the *Taunton Courier* managed to see a link between

Emma's assailant and Jack the Ripper, for one headline referred to it being a Copycat Murder – and Emma Jane was only 9-
years-old when she died.

Major Blake, the local landowner and employer of Mr
Davey, gave milk to those of his workers who cared to collect
it. Each morning Emma Jane took a metal can and went to collect the family's milk supply before going to school or out to
play. The morning of 2 January was no exception; she left
home about 8am, collected the milk from Bridge House, and
wasn't seen alive again. At first Mrs Davey wasn't worried by
Emma Jane's delayed return – it was still the Christmas holiday break from school – but finally she decided something
might be wrong and, together with Emma Jane's 11-year-old
brother Arthur, set out to look for her daughter. About noon
Arthur noticed two white stumps sticking out of a ditch beside a field, and he went to investigate. As he got closer he
saw the mutilated body of his sister. Arthur didn't stay to see
just what had been done to her, he ran shrieking for his
mother, and she ran for help to the local police.

Emma was lying on her back. Her head was embedded in
mud with her mouth and nose under water, as though pres-
sed there. A piece of cord around her neck had been twisted
several times and she had been cut about the throat and other
parts of the body with a razor, and under her body was found
the razor, now broken. Not far from her was the milk can, its
contents spilt across the path, and the can itself dented, with
hair similar in colour to Emma Jane's embedded in the base.

Suspicion fell on Samuel Reyland, a former employee of the
estate. He was a native of Yeabridge, but had left there for
Wales three years previously after being charged with 'attempting to outrage a young girl' whose father also worked
for Major Blake. After Reyland quit the village the parents decided not to press charges. The young man, by then aged 23,
returned to his father's home in the autumn of 1888 and went
to work for his uncle, a road contractor who lived at nearby

Martock. About two hours before the discovery of Emma Jane's body, Mrs Elizabeth Chant had gone along the same path followed by the child and had noticed Reyland standing in the ditch. Soon after she saw him coming towards her, his hat pulled down well over his eyes. She picked him out easily at a police identity parade after Reyland's arrest.

At the trial held at Ilminster Police Court on 12 January, the county analyst reported finding milk spots on Reyland's hat, and said that a hair found on the collar of his coat, when examined under the microscope, matched that of the deceased. The defence made much of the fact that no blood was found on Reyland's clothing and no proof that the milk came from Emma Jane's can, nor that the hair was hers. The Bench committed the accused to the next Assize. Reyland was taken handcuffed to two stalwart constables by train to Exeter Gaol. A large crowd waited at Chard Junction to see and hiss the prisoner en route.

Samuel Reyland pleaded not guilty at the Somerset Assize held at Taunton on 20 February, but was found guilty as charged, and sentenced to hang. Before he died he wrote a letter to his family confessing to the murder and putting it down to the fact that he had been hit on the head with a lump of coal while working at Cardiff, since when he had done several irrational acts. He could give no reason for having behaved as he did towards the child.

His was said to be the first execution to take place at Shepton Mallet Gaol since the execution house was built in 1610, and he died on 13 March 1889.

8

Jack White and His Gibbet

The Sun at Wincanton was a favourite gathering place for some of the rougher elements of the town in the early part of the eighteenth century. One of its habituees was John White, son of Nicholas and Elizabeth White of Wincanton. His exact date of birth is not known, but parish records show that he was baptised on 16 December 1690, his mother died when he was 8 years old and the records also show that he was married to Sarah Slade on 19 May 1716. The events that led to him ending his days on a gibbet took place when he was in his 40th year.

John White was fond of cock fighting, drinking, and talking with his cronies in the ale houses of Wincanton. He had no regular employment and welcomed the chance to earn the occasional shilling. Early in August 1730 he was at the Sun when a man named Robert Sutton called in for a drink and a rest. He was a stranger to the district and had with him an important document that he was charged to deliver. White was being baited by his drinking companions and to get away from their chaffing he got into conversation with Sutton and presently offered to show him the way to the addressee of the document. The two men walked on the high road to a spot just beyond a house known as Abergavenny Cottage. Then the amount of drink he had had that day, combined with the heat of the sun, caught up with White. He lay down and went to sleep under the hedge.

Sutton wandered on along the road, couldn't find his way and so returned to White. He woke him and urged him to continue on their journey. They hadn't progressed very far when two young women came from the opposite direction. In his drunken state White found them irresistible; he kissed and fondled one and tried to greet the other in the same way. She wasn't having any such familiarity and rebuffed him.

Sutton sided with the woman, whereupon he and White began to quarrel furiously. To soothe him, Sutton produced a small copper disc from his pocket saying that it was a golden half guinea to be spent spend once his errand was completed.

The two men reached the Holton-Bratton Seymour-Castle Cary crossroads (now the A371) and there the effect of the beer, the heat and their exertions overtook them both and they sat down. Sutton fell asleep. White, still smarting from Sutton's defence of the woman, and mindful of the 'golden half guinea' seized a stake from the hedge and, according to a report in the *Whitehall Evening Post* of Saturday 8 August, 'knocked him down, beat out one of his Eyes and ran the stick in at his mouth and out at his Neck and much mangled him'. What his thoughts were when he searched the dead man and found that the coin he had killed for was a worthless disc can only be imagined.

The murder caught the popular imagination. Tradition related that White tried to conceal Sutton's body; he shifted it from ditch to gulley and from gulley to pond, but there was a drought in 1730 and White could find insufficient water to cover his victim. Whatever he did or did not do, John White was soon caught and taken before a magistrate at Henstridge, where it was reported he was put on preliminary trial in a summerhouse, and from there sent for trial at the Bridgwater Assizes in August. He was found guilty and sentenced to be hanged at the scene of the crime; the judge then directed that as soon as he was dead his body should be hung up to rot as a warning to travellers.

On Wednesday, 19 August, the sentence was carried out. It was market day at Wincanton, but farmers and dealers deserted the stalls, weavers left their work at Castle Cary and crowds came from all around to hear John White's last words

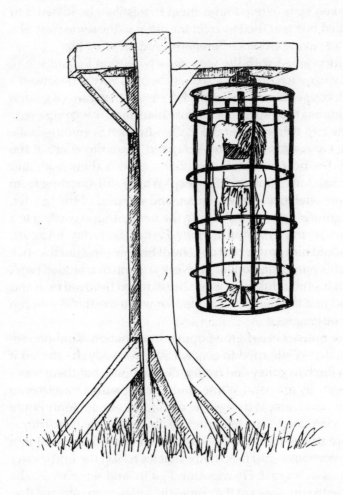

Jack White hanging from a gibbet.

and to watch him die. His body was placed in an iron cage made by the local blacksmith and hoisted into the air on a gibbet. The wooden support was reported as being as large round as an ordinary gate post and about twelve feet high. It was spliced several times at the bottom to keep it intact. It remained in place for many years. From time to time local people would take a splinter from the post to carry as a cure for toothache. Eventually in the 1830s what remained of the gibbet was taken to Galhampton to a beer-house and there burnt, though its site remains recorded on the Ordnance Survey's current maps. The chain from which the cage was suspended disappeared only a short time before.

Possibly because the gibbet served to keep John White's crime alive in the minds of local people many legends grew up around 'Jack' White, and his story became much distorted. He was said to have killed a long-lost brother who had called at the George in Wincanton carrying a large sum of money. Another story had White confessing to the killing of Sutton only after he had been called upon to touch the corpse as it lay in the porch of Wincanton church. Yet another story placed him alive in the iron cage and left to starve to death; a woman was reported to have given him candles to eat, which he'd devoured eagerly. Squire Woodford of Castle Cary after dining rather well at Wincanton had said he was not afraid of the corpse and would even speak to it. He is reported to have asked, 'Well Jack, how be you?' and to his horror he thought he heard the reply, 'Jack's cold – so cold.'

9

The Ladies Aren't for Burning

On 10 May 1790 Sir Benjamin Hammet, Member of Parliament for Taunton, rose in the House of Commons and begged leave to introduce a Bill that would substitute other punishments in lieu of the sentence of burning alive women attainted and convicted of certain crimes (including the killing of a husband). At that time sheriffs who refused to carry out the sentence were liable to be prosecuted, but Sir Benjamin noted that there was not an Englishman alive who would not prefer to risk prosecution rather than torture women so. As a result of his Bill, women sentenced to death after 5 June 1798 were to be hanged, the same as men.

This barbarous custom of burning is indicative of the attitude towards women in the seventeenth and eighteenth centuries – no matter how she might be provoked, beaten or abused, a married woman had no right to leave her husband (if she did she had to leave all her former possessions, including children, with him), and although a man would occasionally escape the death penalty by pleading justifiable homicide if he killed his wife, women, as the 'gentler sex' were expected to be forbearing. It is interesting that there seems to be no word in the English language for a husband killer – other relatives each have a category, parricide (for parents or close relatives), patricide, matricide, infanticide, fratricide, even uxoricide for the killing of a wife – but nothing to describe bumping off the old man. But back to the burning of the ladies; one justification given for the incineration was that it was not fitting that a woman's body should be seen to go through the contortions a man displayed when the noose was tightened around his neck at a public hanging (there was no suggestion then that maybe the public should be barred from watching executions).

The last woman to be burnt in Somerset was Mary Norwood, the 33-year-old wife of Joseph, an Axbridge gardener. She had a great deal to put up with during her marriage and eventually, unable to bear any more abuse, she poisoned him in the spring of 1765. She was taken to the place of execution on 8 May dressed in a garment made of pitch. She was first strangled and then placed on the fire. At her trial she was reported to have been unrepentant but, faced with the large crowd that had assembled to watch her die, she 'asked God for mercy and asked all present to take warning by her shameful death'.

Susannah Bruford before being burnt in 1733

Another lady whose patience was possibly far less than Mary's was Susannah Bruford, who lived near Bridgwater. She was 19 years old and had been married for only three months when she poisoned her husband with arsenic in May 1753. A contemporary account describes how she was taken by sledge to the place of execution at Cure Green, near Wells, dressed in a black gown with a black hood over her head.

There she had prayed for more than half-an-hour with the attending clergyman before she was placed on a stool, known as a trippet. A rope was placed about her neck. She prayed that God would receive her soul. A minute or so later she dropped the black handkerchief she was holding as a signal that the stool should be pushed from under her to let the noose kill her. Two iron plates that surrounded her body were nailed to a stake to keep it upright and a barrel of pitch was set in place to ensure the fire burnt fiercely. Then faggots were heaped over the barrel and around the body and the fire was set. It burnt for nearly an hour. What remained of Susannah was placed in a small coffin for her friends to take away and bury.

According to the parish register of West Monkton, a man named John Bruford was buried at West Monkton on 7 June, 1753, and he was possibly Susannah's husband. The Bruford family lived at Creechbarrow, Bathpool, and there is a record of marriage at Durleigh on 5 March, 1753, but what caused Susannah to kill her husband, after so short a time together, is not known. Poison, while easier to obtain in those days, was never the means by which unpremeditated killings took place, so it was unlikely to have been a spur-of-the-moment affair.

By the time Sarah Freeman was indicted for murder, burning of women had been ended for 55 years, but Sarah's crimes were such that might have justified so horrible a sentence, although she was actually sentenced for the murder of her brother. Whether there was cause to suspect her of the murder of her husband Henry Freeman before she embarked on a series of killings (including that of her child), I have been unable to discover, but Henry died in December 1843, leaving Sarah, aged about 26, to cope with raising their son James. She went first to live with her parents, people called Dimond, at their home in Shapwick, but in the following September left to take up residence with her in-laws at Bridgwater. By

December she was back at Shapwick again, begging to be allowed to return to live with the family. Her brother, Charles, in whose name the tied cottage seems to have been held, was adamant that Sarah should not be allowed to remain, claiming that he would lose his job if she did. Their mother, Mary Dimond, persuaded Charles that Sarah should stay just briefly until she'd found alternative accommodation and proceeded to make up a bed for the young woman.

The following Sunday, Mrs Dimond died; Sarah stayed on to cook for the menfolk. Charles was still reluctant to give her houseroom (there was a suggestion that he was planning to marry). Soon after Christmas he died, having been the only member of the family to eat the herring and boiled potatoes prepared for him on Boxing Day (a Thursday). He was quite sick, and to help his recovery Sarah gave him gruel, which only made him worse. He died at 5am on the following Tuesday. As the indictment mentions only the death of Charles Dimond, I've not found out when young James died, but her old father and her brother John remained to testify at her trial at the 1845 Spring Assizes held in Taunton.

The murders were premeditated affairs. Early in December Sarah had gone to the premises of Mr Vardon, a Bridgwater druggist, to buy a quantity of arsenic. The apprentice who served her (a young man named William Hare) refused at first to let her have any, but she told him that she was the sister of Edmund Durston, the local postman, and this seems to have been a sufficient recommendation for procuring a half ounce of arsenic, divided between two paper packages. Mr Durston happened to be passing the shop as Sarah emerged and she persuaded him to allow her to drive with him part of the way back to Shapwick.

Mr Herapath, an analytical chemist living in Bristol, carried out a post mortem examination of various organs belonging to brother Charles and the *Taunton Courier* of 9 April carried a gruesomely complete account of his findings – enough to say that Charlie had been well and truly poisoned. Despite a plea from the defence that the evidence should be extremely carefully weighed up before passing judgement, the gentlemen of the jury were out for only a quarter-of-an-hour before returning a verdict of Guilty, and Sarah was sentenced to hang. Unlike Charlotte Harris, the 32-year-old wife of William Harris, who was found guilty at the next assize of the murder by poison of Henry Marchant, Sarah received no reprieve, and her execution on 23 April, 1845, was watched by some 7,000 persons.

The case of Charlotte Harris proved interesting when followed up in the newspaper files. She had been the wife of Henry Marchant, a 28-year-old quarryman. The couple lived in a room at Angel Place, Lower Bristol Road, Bath, with their little daughter aged 3. It seemed to be a happy enough marriage; Henry was generous to his wife, allowing her 12/- a week housekeeping money, and the newspaper report commented that the family lived in comfort 'for their station in life'.

On Saturday, 31 March 1849, Henry had stayed out drinking beer with a workmate until midnight, and when he came home Charlotte made him a cup of tea. An hour later he was seized by violent stomach pains and began to vomit. He went to work on the Monday morning, but felt so ill he had to go home to bed. A local doctor called and treated him for a diseased stomach (gastritis). Henry died on the following Saturday and was buried on Friday, 13 April.

The bereaved Charlotte left her lodging on Monday, 16 April, and the neighbours noticed she had bought herself a new dress. Then the news flashed round Angel Place – Widow Marchant had remarried that same day. Her new husband was William Harris, a retired market gardener. Mr Harris had obviously seen better days – he went to his wedding in a wheel chair and despite the fact that he and his bride had wanted a quiet ceremony, there was a fairly large crowd outside. Mr Harris had buried two wives already within the past year, though the blame for neither death cannot be laid at his door. His first wife and he had been happily married for nearly 50 years. To ease the gap left in his life, after her death in 1848, William married a young woman named Louisa Perry in the following June. She lived only until February 1849, being of a delicate disposition.

Mr Harris was reported to have been disappointed with the amount of money left by Louisa, and there was some speculation as to whether her death really was due to natural causes, but this was quickly quashed.

The speed of Charlotte's remarriage caused the police to dig up Henry Marchant's body and to consult William Herapath, the Bristol-based analytical chemist. He soon found that someone had adminstered some hefty doses of arsenic to Henry, and it wasn't long before Charlotte Harris was arrested and brought for trial.

Investigations showed that the accused had been an orange seller before her first marriage; she was described in those days as being a 'woman of loose habits' and had been previously in court charged with knocking down a woman (who subsequently died because her head hit the gutter in her fall) and robbing her of a shawl. A shocked William Harris told the court that he did not realise that his wife was a recent widow, she had told him nothing about Henry Marchant.

The trial took one and a half days; some 40 witnesses were examined and the jury didn't take long to find Charlotte Harris guilty of murder, and she was sentenced to hang. Then the defence sprang a surprise – the prisoner was pregnant. The judge ordered that a panel of twelve ladies should be chosen to examine Mrs Harris (one can imagine the hubbub in court). Her pregnancy established, Mr Justice Creswell ordered that the sentence be respited. It is to be hoped that Charlotte Harris cherished that child throughout her lifelong sentence of transportation.

Finally, in this account of ladies who committed murder we come to Catherine Churchill who went to the scaffold protesting her innocence at a time when the fear of God in this life and of the Judgment Throne in the next were enough to draw a confession from all but the most hardened of criminals. Catherine Churchill was not a hardened criminal though; she was a woman of 50, and one whose life had been hard.

As a girl, young Kitty Waldron (as Catherine Churchill was then) was very attractive and could probably have taken her pick of the village lads – in fact she did take her pick, but the lad she chose had his fun and left her holding the baby, a little girl. There is no mention in the records of who the father was, nor of what happened to the child. In the mid-nineteenth century an illegitimate baby almost certainly put paid to any hopes a woman might have of marriage to someone other than the father.

Then Samuel Churchill's wife died. I haven't been able to discover what Samuel did for a living, but he owned a small cottage at Knowle St Giles some 300 yards from the Ilminster-to-Chard railway line (this fact was to feature in the subsequent trial). He was about 57 years old and accustomed to his creature comforts. His only daughter was married and so Kitty was invited, almost immediately following the bereavement, to the Churchill cottage, presumably to act as a housekeeper.

It is likely that Samuel soon decided that Kitty should cater to all his needs and within a couple of years she gave birth to a son who was named Samuel Waldron (children of unwed parents usually carried the mother's surname, although this was not true of Charles Bampfylde's illegitimate son who features in another story in this book). The couple continued to live together, and although there was no reason why they should not marry, Samuel held out against making an honest woman of Kitty until 1870, when he was 73. Kitty had her wedding ring at long last. With the couple and their son lived

Kitty's mother, old Mrs Waldron, who was as deaf as a post. That deafness was to have a profound effect upon Kitty's fate.

Despite achieving respectability in marriage, life for Kitty became even more difficult. Samuel was not a good husband; he was often cruel and never complimentary about anything his wife did for him. Kitty, for her part, was not one to lie down meekly under her husband's tirades, and neighbours often heard them shouting at each other. Young Samuel eventually moved out and went into service. He kept in touch with his mother, but appears to have had little to do with his father.

With such frequent squabbles it isn't surprising, therefore, when on 4 March 1879 Mrs Eliza Whatley heard groans and cries of 'Murder' coming from the Churchill cottage she took no notice. Questioned by the police, she said that while she was on her way to take her carter husband his breakfast she saw a woman pushing with her hands at something heavy within the house. Later that morning, at about 10:30, Catherine Churchill ran across the field to George Whatley and asked him to come quickly to her home. She said she had just come home and had found her husband fallen in the fire after having one of his fits. Mr Whatley went in and saw the old man on his back beside the fire, which had burned low. He was dead. He had been severely burned about the head, one ear was burnt away and one shoulder was singed to the bone.

The police came to the house and during their investigation found various articles of bloodstained clothing; there were also some newly washed garments including a woman's dress and a house cloth. Churchill's pipe had blood on it, there was also a bloodstained billyhook on which the detective found one human hair. A wound on the dead man's hand was still bleeding when he was discovered. Catherine said she had gone to the Ship Inn to buy bread and bacon that morning. She had left soon after the train went by and at that time her husband was sitting at the left side of the fire smoking a pipe. When found, the head was at the left side of the fire and the legs pointed toward the right side, an impossible position if Samuel had toppled from his chair into the fire (but as he could move around, no one seems to have thought that he just might have stood up and walked to the other side of the fireplace).

Catherine Churchill was charged with murder, appearing before the Ilminster magistrates on 13 March 1879. Much of the case against her rested on the evidence of Elizabeth Whatley; she agreed that the old man was tottery, citing a time several months before Christmas when he had gone to her house and collapsed on the step when she opened the door. Catherine Churchill had been called and left without him, saying it served the old rogue right and she wished he were dead. For the past few months, though, the couple had seemed to be more friendly toward each other. Mrs Whatley denied that the accused had gone out at the time she said (the signalman, Frederick Newton, told the court the train went through at 9am) because she heard the key turn in the door and thought she saw Catherine upstairs.

A local surgeon, Charles Munden, confirmed that he had treated Samuel for fainting fits and said that Mrs Churchill had recently called in for a repeat of the medicine. Dr Munden thought the old man might easily have become dizzy and fallen into the fire, and when asked how come the deceased was lying so awkwardly, he said that possibly the old man had moved to try and get away from the fire and had then collapsed in the position found.

The magistrates decided Catherine should appear at the Somerset Assizes and she was admitted to Shepton Mallet Gaol to await trial (the Gaol Records note that she was literate and a washerwoman by trade). She appeared on 3 May before A.J. Collins.

Catherine's defence pointed out that the Churchills kept

pigs and chickens, and the blood on the clothing and the billyhook could easily have come from them; as for the old
man's pipe, medical evidence was produced to show that it
was not unusual for the gums of an old person to bleed and
the blood might well have been there because of natural
bleeding. Samuel Churchill was accustomed to chop wood
for the fire and could have injured his hand while cutting
some up the previous day. Catherine's old mother spent her
days in bed upstairs and because of her extreme deafness had
heard nothing of what happened, making it impossible to call
her as a witness for the defence (might she have been the
woman Elizabeth Whatley saw at the window?).

The prosecution brought forth Mr Stoddart, the county
analyst. He said the bloodstains in the seams of Mrs
Churchill's dress were consistent with the dragging of a
heavy body forcing blood into the seams. Witnesses testified
that they had noticed no wound on Samuel Churchill's hand
when they saw him the day before he died. Eleven-year-old
Ellen Hart was called and told the court that as she made her
way to school at 9:30 on 4 March she noticed a smell from the
Churchill's cottage which 'stinked terrible'. This, the prosecution suggested, was the smell of the body burning.

The old man's will was produced; he had left £5 to his
daughter and the remainder of his property to Samuel Waldron with the proviso that his wife should occupy the cottage
throughout her lifetime and that if his son died without issue
during Catherine's lifetime, his daughter should inherit everything. The managing clerk to the Chard solicitors told the
court that Catherine had been to see him the previous
November to ask about the terms of the will, but he had told
her that without the old man's permission he could tell her
nothing. The prosecution alleged that Samuel Churchill had
threatened to alter his will and disinherit this son and to prevent this, Catherine had killed him. It was argued in support
of this theory that, when he was found, Samuel was wearing

his best breeches, something he would never have done unless he intended to visit Chard and someone of consequence – such as his lawyer (presumably in those days it was not the custom to make an appointment to see such a person, otherwise, surely the lawyer would have been called either as a defence or as a prosecution witness).

The jury retired, spent one and a quarter hours in deliberation and then came back to ask whether there was any evidence that the old man had struck his wife first. Hearing that there was no such evidence, the foreman immediately gave the verdict of 'Guilty as charged'. An appeal by the Knowle rector's wife for clemency for Catherine, in light of the cruelty shown her by Samuel over the years, was turned down.

Poor unhappy Catherine was executed in the van house facing the Shire Hall at the extreme west angle of Taunton Prison shortly after 8am on 28 May 1879. Her body lies in an unmarked grave in the precincts of the gaol.

10
Death of a Rake?

Sir Charles Bampfylde had his detractors and he also had his defenders, so whether his death is seen as Divine Retribution or as a sad occurrence depends upon which authority is consulted.

Sir Charles, as a young man, had been a close companion of the Prince Regent and gained a reputation for being a dissolute rake. He succeeded to the Bampfylde title and the estates that included much of the Somerset village of Hardington Bampfylde in 1776. There was not much income with his inheritance and as the great country house that his ancestors had occupied had largely been destroyed by fire, leaving only a comparatively small wing to be run, Sir Charles tended to spend more and more time there to keep down his expenses. The estate was fairly remote and became popular as a weekend retreat for the circle with whom Bampfylde had spent his debauched youth. He had not been averse to sowing wild oats in his time — and did acknowledge at least one of his illegitimate offspring, a son.

The boy was also named Charles Bampfylde and when he reached maturity he took Holy Orders and was appointed rector of Hemington and Hardington by his father, who had the living in his gift. Incidentally, the Rev Charles was known as the 'Devil of Dunkerton' (another of his parishes) and was said to be so enthusiastic a huntsman that he frequently took the services in his church wearing his riding boots and breeches under his clerical robes. When the time came each year for the collection of tithes, the Rev Charles sat with a brace of loaded pistols on the table beside him as a warning to potential robbers (and possibly to encourage extraction of the dues). The Rev John Skinner, whose *Journal of a Somerset Rector* was most scathing about Sir Charles, was equally scathing about the son 'To see the bastard son of such a father having the same inclination and the same principles, sitting as a magistrate to determine on the actions of his fellow creatures, and as a clergyman to preach against immorality and irreligion; this is indeed a melancholy token of the decadance of the times'.

Sir Charles eventually settled down and had a legitimate family, but possibly his eye continued to wander because on 9 April 1823, in his 71st year, *The Times* published an item with the heading 'Attempted Murder of Sir Charles Bampfylde'. Apparently, on 7 April, while staying at his London house at 1, Montague Square, Sir Charles had been approached by a man who attempted to assassinate him with a pistol and who then drew another pistol and shot himself dead. The assailant was identified as Joseph Morland whose wife had lived with the Bampfylde family.

At the coroner's inquest held at the Worcester Arms on George Street, Portman Square, Lucy Stockey, wife of a coachman, Thomas Stockey, gave evidence that she was friendly with Morland's wife who 'lived in the service of Sir Charles' (she was a housekeeper). Morland himself was a footman with another household. Lucy Stockey sold fruit at the corner of Montague Street almost opposite the Bampfylde residence. Joseph Morland had spoken to her frequently in the three weeks before the attack took place. He had been wanting to see Sir Charles before standing trial on 8 April for assault because he hoped to persuade Sir Charles to forbid his servant to testify against him. (The reporter did not disclose against whom the assault took place or for what reason.) Morland remained talking with Mrs Stockey on the fateful day until he saw Sir Charles approaching and then he left her. She saw nothing more until she heard the pistol shot and then Sir Charles came toward her saying 'The villain has shot me.'

The Times was silent on the subject for a couple of weeks and then on 24 April ran a column entitled 'Killed in a Duel'. The coroner's inquest, with Sir William Keir Grant as foreman of the jury and Thomas Stirling as coroner, was held on 23 April at 1 Montague Square at the request of the family, despite the fact that the body was soldered up in its coffin.

There were so many rumours flying around that the Bampfyldes wanted an inquiry into just why Morland killed Sir Charles. Dr Henry Ainslie of Dover Street, Picadilly said that he had been sent for on 12 April and had found Sir Charles in bed. He had a very quick pulse but was free from fever and composed in his mind. Ainslee visited the house twice daily and until 18 April there was no sign of the patient becoming worse. Following Sir Charles's death on the 19th, Ainslee attended the examination of the body and found a pistol bullet sticking between two ribs. Apparently the bullet had taken its course through the back and had broken a rib and part of the spine. The inflammation that followed was the immediate cause of death. Ainslee made no mention of any other foreign body being present in the corpse, but according to the book on Hardington Bampfylde Church written by Michael McGarvie (published by the Redundant Churches Fund in 1978) a piece of wire that formed part of the spring of the baronet's braces was thrust into the body by the entry of the bullet, could not be extracted and so corroded and caused gangrene within the wound – obviously one of the rumours the family was attempting to dispel has remained.

The next person to be called at the inquest was Benjamin Hopewell of 60 George Street. He identified himself as an apothecary and said that he had been sent for at about 4.30 in the afternoon of 7 April and had found Sir Charles standing up in his dressing room in a state of considerable agitation. Examination showed a wound three inches below the shoulder blade on the right side of the back. Hopewell ordered Sir Charles to be put to bed and to be kept quiet until the surgeon

Mr Heaviside arrived. Hopewell continued to attend Sir Charles until he died. Sir William Grant asked whether any other substances were found with the bullet and was told 'part of his flannel jacket', which was removed immediately.

Hopewell confirmed Lucy Stockey's evidence given at Morland's inquest that an assault charge was pending against Joseph Morland and he said it was being brought by Sir Charles's servants. Morland had asked him to forego the prosecution and Sir Charles said he'd have nothing to do with him and to be about his business. Then Sir Charles had felt a sudden pain in his back as if from a violent blow and on looking round saw his assailant bleeding at the mouth.

Thomas Jones, John Longhurst and Lucy Stockey were called to prove Morland had fired the pistol. Mrs Stockey was questioned by the foreman of the jury and said she'd not had much conversation with Morland that day, but he seemed to be in low spirits. Asked if he appeared to be a bad man, she seems to have avoided answering directly by saying only that she had known him for eight years. Questioned about his attempt to get Sir Charles to stop the prosecution she confirmed that Morland wanted it stopped so that he might get a job. Sir William Grant said he understood Morland to be engaged as a butler at York Place. The reporter made no comment about that remark, but presumably if the case had proceeded Morland knew he would be dismissed.

Having established that Morland fired the bullet and that both he and Sir Charles were dead, there wasn't much that the coroner's inquest could do but adjourn. Sir Charles Bampfylde was buried at Hardington Bampfylde in the family vault at the chancel end of the church. The service was conducted by a clergyman who lived at nearby Ammerdown, the Rev J.R. Jolliffe. Two sons were in attendance (one wonders whether one was the Rev Charles and whether he was too upset by his father's death to conduct the service himself) and a few of his intimate neighbours along with 'a vast body of his tenantry, eager to pay the last tribute of respect to the memory of one who also proved himself a most kind and liberal landlord'. The same writer also described him as a 'generous and indulgent parent, the life and soul of every social circle, and whose loss will be most deeply deplored.'

Sir Charles is just another example of the truth of Shakespeare's statement that 'the evil that men do lives after them, the good is oft interred with their bones'. It is far more dramatic to portray him as a libertine who was avenged by a wronged husband than as just an elderly gentleman who became involved with someone else's hot-headed servant.

Hardington Bampfylde church, burial place of Sir Charles Bampfylde.

11

The Motiveless Murder

This case is one of the few where there is considerable information available about the family and all those involved both before and after the murder occurred – and that rarely happened in the days before instant communication. Local folk would know the victim and perpetrator, but without reporters on hand to note down what happened, events soon were forgotten or, worse, were embroidered upon and became the stuff of legend.

Murder is always sordid; generally there is a motive, or even several motives, that help to lead investigators to the criminal. It may be that a spouse is unfaithful, or has abused a partner beyond human endurance. Over-indulgence in alcohol has led to many an argument and a fight that wouldn't have happened had the participants been sober. Fear of discovery in a lesser crime is another reason for killing, and greed features in many cases.

Occasionally, though, a murder is motiveless. Such a slaying was that of Francis Savill Kent in June 1860. He was less than four years old (admittedly some four-year-olds can behave very badly, but rarely badly enough to provoke actual murder) and from all accounts this little boy was sunny natured and inspired warmth in those around him. On the night of 29 June, 1860, someone took that little boy, sleeping, from his cot, wrapped him in the under-blanket from his bed and carried him downstairs and out of the house. Then that someone cut his throat and stuffed his body into an outside earth privy. All members of the household were questioned, and all denied knowledge of the deed, claiming to have been asleep throughout the night.

The household was composed of seven adults (eight, if you include 16-year-old Constance Kent) and three children, apart from the victim. Mrs Kent was in the final weeks of her fourth pregnancy and was forced to rest as much as possible.

The child's father, Samuel Savill Kent, was a sub-inspector of factories, and anxious to rise in his profession. In 1826 he met a successful coach builder named Thomas Windus and became friendly with the family. In January 1829 Mary Anne Windus, the eldest daughter, was married to Samuel. Their first son, Thomas, was born less than a year later and died in January 1831. Then came two daughters, Mary Anne and Elizabeth, both of whom grew to adulthood and remained at home. In 1835 Edward Windus Kent was born; possibly by then the family was living at Sidmouth in Devon, but Edward was educated at Crewkerne in Somerset and at the age of 14 was sent to the naval school at Gosport. Meanwhile between February 1837 and April 1842, Mrs Kent gave birth to four more babies, all of whom died before they were a year old. It isn't surprising that, by the time the last child died, Mrs Kent was exhibiting signs of mental instability, but that didn't prevent her giving birth in February 1844 to Constance Emily and in July 1845 to William Savill.

While the family was at Sidmouth in 1839 Samuel Kent engaged Mary Drewe Pratt as governess to his children. The daughter of a Devon grocer, she was 19 and quite attractive (Mr Kent was known to be susceptible to the ladies, in fact it was said later that some 200 maidservants passed through his household, many of whom were pursued by the master). Following William's birth, Mr Kent moved out of his wife's room and into the one beside that of Mary Pratt. As a result there was much gossip in the town. Mr Kent also spent well above his means and eventually there was an interview with the Factory Commissioner as a result of which, in 1848, the family left Sidmouth and moved to Walton near Clevedon (then in Somerset).

By then Mary Anne Kent had been replaced as mistress of the house by the governess. Constance had been virtually brought up by Mary Pratt and hardly knew her own mother. Gossip again circulated in the village and in March 1852 the household moved once more, this time to Baynton House, East Coulston in Wiltshire. Mary Pratt's father was sick and she left on 1 May for Devonshire. Next day Mrs Kent became ill with severe stomach pains and, despite medical attention, died on 5 May. Mary Pratt hurried back to be with the family and was present at the burial at East Coulston church six days later. On 15 May Mr Pratt died. News of the deaths reached the places where the family had lived previously, and the tongues wagged furiously.

After fifteen months of widowhood, Samuel Kent took Mary Drewe Pratt as his second wife on 11 August, 1853. Constance and her two older sisters were in attendance as bridesmaids. Possibly to avoid the gossip mongers the ceremony took place at St Mary's Church, Lewisham, the bride having managed somehow to register as being resident in the district. Edward Kent, the first surviving son of Mary Anne was at sea when the marriage occurred and, upon coming home on leave and learning of the affair, he was so enraged that he left the house immediately and returned to his ship. Eventually father and son were reconciled.

1854 was a sad year for the Kents; Mary gave birth to a stillborn child in June and in November came news that Edward had died when his ship, *Kenilworth*, had gone down with all hands off the Crimean coast. Mr Kent, griefstricken, haunted the Admiralty in his efforts to find out more about the circumstances of the disaster, but to no avail. A month later, as he and his wife were stepping into the carriage on their way to Bath to buy mourning clothes, the postman arrived with a letter from Edward bearing the happy news that he had survived the shipwreck.

The next summer Mary Amelia was born. By then, having

found that Baynton House was extremely costly to support and furthermore, that the gossip concerning his wife's former status was proving a barrier to the social acceptance that he craved, Samuel Kent took a lease on Road Hill House near Frome, at the north eastern border of Somerset. Constance and William were packed off to boarding school in January 1856, but because of the expense their father removed them after only two terms.

Constance especially was upset at the thought of once more being educated by Mrs Kent and she persuaded William to join her in running away. Constance cut off her hair and dressed in some of her brother's old clothing. The two then walked the ten miles to Bath and sought a night's lodging at the Greyhound Hotel. The innkeeper, becoming suspicious, questioned the children and took William to the police station where the boy confessed all. Mr Kent realised that the home situation was becoming intolerable and once more the chil-

Road Hill House, near Frome.

dren were sent to boarding school, and the one chosen this time for 12-year-old Constance ensured that she rarely came home for the holidays (although both she and William were home on the night of the murder).

Francis Savill, known to his family as Savill, was born in August 1856. He was the delight of his mother and the joy of his father, but just before his second birthday, the father's joy was tempered by the news that Edward had died on board the *Clyde*, of yellow fever, and this time there was to be no re-prieve. He left about £300, of which one third each went to Mary Anne and Elizabeth and the remaining third was to be divided equally between Constance and William.

Road Hill House (Road is now spelt 'Rode') was large and had several spare rooms, but for some reason few members of the household slept separately. On the top (second) floor were two spare rooms as well as bedrooms for Mary Anne and Elizabeth, who also shared a bed; Sarah Kerslake, the cook, slept with Sarah Cox, the housemaid (maybe they were placed together by Mrs Kent who was mindful of the goings on before she married); Constance and William, then aged 15, were the only ones to have separate accommodation. The pa-rents slept on the first floor with five-year-old Mary Amelia in with them and nearby the children's nursemaid shared a bed-room with Francis Savill and his two-year-old sister Evelina.

Following the discovery of Savill's murder, Elizabeth Gough testified that she had been nurse to the Kents for eight months. Savill was a cheerful and happy child and had been put to bed at 8pm. That particular day he had been in the charge of his father while the female members of the house-hold had been busy with spring cleaning. Elizabeth Gough went to bed, exhausted, at 11pm. At about 5am she awoke, noticed that Savill was not in his cot, assumed that his mother had come in and taken him into her bed (and this, despite the fact that one reason Mr Kent had been caring for Savill was because he was too heavy for the pregnant Mrs Kent to lift), and so she turned over and slept again. An hour later she knocked on the parents' door and asked whether the boy was with them. A search of the house showed that the drawing room window was partly open and a search of the grounds was made. The Kents had a Newfoundland watchdog that was let loose in the grounds by night, but (according to her) he hadn't been heard to bark at all.

The situation was rather awkward for the police. At that time, although Road itself was in Somerset, Road Hill House was within the Wiltshire boundary (it has since been included in Somerset). PC Urch of the Somerset Constabulary said that he was on duty that night and he did hear Mr Kent's dog bark furiously about 1am (Joe Moon and another man also said they heard the barking, but as they were poaching Mr Kent's trout from the River Frome at the time, understandably they weren't all that keen on letting him know how they came to hear the dog. Joe Moon's brother had already been before the magistrates, charged with trespass by Mr Kent, so maybe there was little love between the families). But the Wiltshire Police took control and PC Urch's evidence was not entered in the initial investigation.

According to later reports, Samuel Kent showed little anxiety when Savill was first reported missing; he stayed in bed and didn't join in the search. When he did dress and go downstairs he said that someone must have stolen the child and had his carriage prepared so that he might drive off to Trowbridge to report to the police (although other police were nearer at hand). Meanwhile, others who were not so sure about the possibility of kidnap continued to search the grounds and the house.

Savill was found by Thomas Benger, described as a yeoman of Road. He said that after searching the shrubbery for the child he had noticed dark coloured blood on the floor of the privy and after lifting the lid he had sent for a light and found the body, dressed in a nightshirt, lying across the splashboard. The splashboard was to figure later when some members of the Press were seeking to lay the blame for the murder on Mr Kent, for it was he who had ordered its installation and would have known that it would prevent the body sinking into the cesspit below.

Benger wrapped the body in the under-blanket, which was lying nearby, and carried it through to the kitchen. The child's face was peaceful, there was no sign of a struggle, but his head had nearly been severed from his body by a knife or some other sharp instrument. A piece of flannel was found nearby; the laundress, when sent for and questioned, was unable to identify it as coming from any of the clothing that she washed for the family. Stephen Milett, the local butcher and parish constable of Road, found a bloodstained newspaper nearby and about two tablespoonsful of blood on the privy floor. Elizabeth Gough told the men that she didn't recognise the paper – the household took *The Times*, the *Civil Service Gazette* and a Frome newspaper.

At the inquest held at the Red Lion a Dr Parsons said that he had examined the body and found that a sharp pointed knife also had been used to stab the left side of the chest just below the nipple. There was a blackened, bruised appearance around the mouth. This latter statement, although confirmed by several witnesses, was ignored by the coroner. Dr Parsons also said that he believed the child to have been smothered by pressure of a soft substance over the mouth, but as he made that statement after he had been excused by the coroner, this was not entered on the deposition. The small amount of blood found where the body was deposited would have been consistent with death taking place before the mutilation of the body.

Sarah Cox, the housemaid, stated that one of her duties was to fasten the windows, shutters and doors at the front of the house before she went to bed at night. Her master and mistress had still been up when she went to bed on the night of Friday, 29 June, but she had performed the locking up as required. Next morning at 6.05am she found the drawing room door open and the shutters and windows slightly ajar. Samuel Kent testified that he had checked the locks before he went to bed and had found all secure. He claimed that the murder was an act of revenge by a villager or by a discharged domestic servant (don't forget that estimate of 200 women servants passing through the household). The male staff comprised a gardener/coachman who had been with the family for some years and a boy who cleaned the knives and shoes and who was under notice to leave the following day. Both slept out and therefore were not suspect.

Because Road was so near to the Wiltshire border, police from both counties were involved in the investigation. Much was made of the fact that one of Constance's nightgowns was missing. According to a later report, Sgt Watts of the Somerset Constabulary mentioned to the enquiry officer, Mr Saunders, that he had found a bloodstained 'nightshift' secreted in a boiler hole in the back kitchen. Two Wiltshire policemen, Messrs Foley and Dallimore, passed over the evidence lightly saying that the garment had been shown to the police surgeon who said that the bloodstains came from natural causes. Later the surgeon denied being shown the nightshift.

Constance was suspected of having committed the crime but was then discharged. Next, Elizabeth Gough was accused and she was discharged also. After that the Press began a smear campaign against Samuel Kent, pointing to the number of his children who had died and suggesting that their deaths too might have been caused by unnatural means. Eventually interest in the case died down and apart from a book, Stapleton's *The Great Crime of 1860* (published in 1861 by E. Marlborough & Co of London), the Road Hill House murder was forgotten.

Interest revived in 1865 when *The Times* of 22 July reported that Constance Emilie Kent had been indicted for the 'wilful

murder of Francis Savill Kent at Road-hill-house on the 29th
June 1860.' All the old gossip was renewed, and more added.

Constance wore deep mourning and a thick veil for her
trial. She spoke first with her solicitor Mr Ravenhill and then
put up her veil and went to the front of the dock. When asked
how did she say 'Guilty or Not Guilty', she replied 'Guilty'.
The judge asked her if she was aware she was being charged
with wilfully and intentionally murdering her brother. Did
she plead guilty or not guilty. 'Guilty', was the firm reply. The
judge ordered the plea to be recorded.

Mr Coleridge, QC, who appeared for her, told the court
that Constance wanted it to be known that she was solely responsible for the crime. Her father and others who had for so
long suffered most unjust and cruel suspicions were wholly
and absolutely innocent. She was not driven to the act, as had
been asserted, by unkind treatment at home. There she had
had nothing but tender and forbearing love. The judge then
put on the black cap and after speaking to Constance about allowing jealousy and anger to work in her breast until at last
they assumed over her the influence and power of the evil
one, he sentenced her to death with a suggestion that possibly The Queen would exercise the prerogative of mercy in
view of Constance's youth at the time of the crime.

The trial generated a flood of letters to the newspapers, including one from Inspector Whicher, the detective who arrested Constance in 1861. He concentrated on the missing
nightgown. Constance, he thought, had changed her nightgown in the night and had slept for a while in the clean one
that was shown to the police. He believed she intended to
throw the little boy alive into the cesspit and let him die that
way but, being unable because of the splashboard, had been
forced to use a knife.

The police surgeon, Joseph Whitaker Stapleton, wrote a letter praising Elizabeth Gough for her fidelity to the Kents and
for her unwavering courage and simple truthfulness. She had

been unable to find employment since the murder and Stapleton propos(t that an annuity should be purchased for her with the help of well-wishers (limited to 1 guinea per subscriber). He also suggested the Government might help young William who was nearly 21. Mr Stapleton was quite a writer – he was the author of the book, *The Great Crime of 1860*. In it he had detailed all he knew of the Francis Kent case and had delved into the history of the unfortunate family with all the events that led to the murder, so Constance's confession was of particular interest to him.

Finally, a long letter from John Charles Bucknell, MD, published on 28 August, claimed Constance had told Mr Rodway, her solicitor, the full story of the crime: she had taken a razor from a green case in her father's wardrobe a few days before the murder and had hidden it. This was her only weapon (no mention of the sharp knife). She'd also hidden a candle and matches by putting them in a corner of the closet in the garden. On the night of 29 June she undressed and went to bed, expecting her sister to call in. Soon after midnight she went downstairs and opened the drawing room door and window shutters.

Upstairs she took the blanket from between the sheet and counterpane and placed it on the side of her brother's cot. She then carried the child downstairs and out through the drawing room. She was wearing her nightgown and in the drawing room she put on her galoshes. Holding the child in one arm, she raised the drawing room window and climbed out, going around to the closet. She lighted the candle, then cut the boy's throat as he lay asleep. She thought the blood would never come and he wasn't killed, so she thrust the razor deeper into his throat (no mention of the chest wound). Then she bundled the blanketed body into the vault. The candle burnt out. The flannel that was found nearby was from an old garment in the waste bag that she'd cut up to make washcloths for herself.

When she had returned to her bedroom, she looked at her nightdress, could find only two spots of blood on it and those she'd washed out. She put the nightdress to dry and put on a clean one. In the morning the stained nightdress was dry so she folded it and put it with her clean clothes. Her three nightdresses were examined by the police. When, a few days later, she held the nightdress to the light and could discern the stains, she bundled it up and moved it from place to place, eventually burning it in her bedroom and putting the ashes in the kitchen grate. She had cleaned the razor and replaced it in her father's bedroom during the confusion on the Saturday morning. She said that had Elizabeth Gough been convicted she had made up her mind to confess.

She had liked her stepmother at first but anything that could be seen as disparaging toward her own mother was stored up in her mind. She had felt no animosity towards Francis other than that he was her stepmother's child. She reiterated the statement made in court that she had never been treated unkindly. There are several discrepancies in her account of the murder but the court seems to have accepted it.

The sentence of death passed on Constance Kent was commuted to one of penal servitude for life – which, had she been caught and sentenced in 1860, meant 15 years and that, with good behaviour, she might have been released after 12 years. Constance went to jail unaware that in 1864 the length of time of 'life' had been extended to 20 years. Seven times, from 1877 onward, she petitioned the Home Secretary for release, arguing that the conditions obtaining at the time of her crime should apply. Six times she was refused freedom and then, in 1885, when the petition she presented showed her utter despair, she was released on ticket of leave on 18 July.

The probable reason for the previous refusals was the nature of her crime. During her incarceration the matrons of the various prisons in which she was housed all reported that she was regarded by the inmates with dislike, even with loathing.

The other prisoners shunned her – she had sinned against a child and to this day child molesters and murderers often have to be safeguarded from fellow inmates. Constance worked in the laundry, she also helped in the infirmary during a typhoid outbreak – which may have sown the seeds for her later career. Her 'gentle breeding' set her somewhat apart from most female criminals and at some time during her sentence she did some artwork – mosaics made by her were incorporated into the decoration of the Bishop's Chapel at Chichester Cathedral, St Peter's Church, Portland, in Dorset (known as the convict's church) and several other churches in Britain.

Constance's brother William, the person who meant most to her, had meanwhile sought to make a life for himself. He changed his name to Saville-Kent and in 1872 married. His wife Elizabeth died three years later aged 25; the following year William married Mary Ann Livesey and in 1884 the couple sailed for Tasmania, taking with them Mary Amelia Kent, the oldest of Mary Drewe Kent's children (Mrs Kent herself had died in August 1866 of congestion of the lungs; she was only 46 years old. Samuel Kent lived until February 1872 when he died of liver disease. He and his second wife are buried at Llangollen). William returned to England on business in 1885 and took the recently released Constance (to be known in future as Ruth Emilie Kaye) back with him.

Presumably Ruth Emilie realised that she needed to make her own life and not be too dependent upon her brother and sister-in-law, because in 1890, at the age of 46 she left Tasmania and began the two year training course for nurses at the Alfred Hospital in Melbourne.

She then worked with lepers until, in 1898, she became matron of a Perth institute for girls in trouble. Twelve years later, having had several nursing posts, Ruth leased a hostel for nurses in a Sydney suburb and remained as its matron until she was 88, staying on as a resident for several years after her retirement. Her 100th birthday in February 1944 was marked by telegrams from King George VI and Queen Elizabeth and the Lieutenant Governor of the State; the Archbishop of Sydney called on her and the local newspapers made much of this 'much beloved lady' who had served the community so well and for so long (reporters were told she arrived in Australia 20 years before she actually did).

Two months later, the woman who had been so notorious in mid-Victorian England, died. The full story, some of which must be classed as conjecture, is contained in Bernard Taylor's book, *Cruelly Murdered*, but rarely has any crime generated interest that has continued until this day, and rarely has a criminal been able to expiate the deed so fully.

12

Yet Each Man Kills the Thing He Loves

The majority of murders are domestic, one spouse disposes of the other. Usually a husband is the perpetrator although, as this book proves, several women killed their husbands – usually by poison, which gives credence to the belief that poison is a woman's weapon. But statistically far more men sent their spouses to an untimely grave.

The last public execution at Taunton took place in 1867 when George Britten, a native of Wolverton, near Frome, was hanged for beating his wife Martha to death on 18 July. He had then tried to conceal the crime by burning the body. He was a 51 year-old farmer and presumably had been married for some years. His final contact with his family was when his brother-in-law visited him in prison to receive instructions on the upbringing of the couple's son. The High Sheriff of Somerset tried to keep the date of execution secret because he felt the depraved taste for wanting to witness such a sickening sight should not be pandered to.

Usually executions took place on a Tuesday in Taunton and several hundred people, many of them from outlying villages, assembled outside Wilton Gaol on 27 August. They were disappointed; no hanging took place that day. An appeal had been launched for clemency as Britten had expressed his profound detestation of the crime and had acknowledged that his punishment was just. On the Wednesday the crowds were again disappointed. Finally, the appeal having failed, on Thursday, 29 August, Britten was hanged before fewer than 200 witnesses. A pit filled with quicklime had been prepared within the prison grounds and, a few minutes after his death, he was buried.

The farmhouse at Cannington where Thomas Michell murdered his wife and sister-in-law in 1539.

Compared with the crowd of 3,000 who came in 1844 to watch Taunton's first public hanging in 44 years, the spectacle was obviously losing its appeal. That 1844 execution was of another husband, Joel Fisher, who had murdered his wife at the Devonshire Inn, Weston-super-Mare. Fisher was an old soldier who had fought under the Duke of Wellington in Spain and at Waterloo. One of his guards was a fellow soldier from the same regiment, the 7th Hussars, and possibly he arranged for several of Fisher's former comrades to attend him at the last.

Not every known murderer ends up on the scaffold, although in this particular case the spotlight rested more upon property than upon the unfortunate victims. It concerned Thomas Michell, a wealthy farmer who lived at Cannington. On 13 December 1539 he murdered his wife Joan and her sister, Eleanor Sydenham, a widow, and then committed suicide. In those days a felon's property was forfeit to the Crown; there were two sons of the Michell marriage, 15-year-old Richard and his younger brother John, and presumably for their sakes Sir Thomas Warre, the next of kin of the two sisters, is alleged to have taken possession of the Michell goods and to have ordered burial of the bodies. The coroner is required by law to visit the scene of the crime and to conduct an inquest into precisely what happened. You'd have thought that three dead persons, with a suspicion of murder in two of those deaths, would have brought a coroner rushing to the scene, but William Picher of Crewkerne didn't reach Cannington for three days – according to his report twelve men died on the same day and he couldn't go to see all of them immediately.

By the time he arrived, practically all of Michell's movable property (valued then at £1,000) had vanished. At first the jury found that lack of sufficient evidence existed to warrant bringing in a verdict of suicide in the case of Thomas Michell, although they were all agreed that he had committed murder. They were due to meet again at Bridgwater to consider their verdict on 5 January 1540, but William Picher sent word to John Sheares, the bailiff of Cannington, to say he was ill and to request a few days' delay to the proceedings. Then the jurymen excused themselves on another day because of their work as watermen, so that by the time the final verdict of suicide was handed down, the dispersal of goods was complete.

The Star Chamber, originally set up to counteract corruption of judges and juries, examined the evidence and ruled that a proper inventory should be made of all goods belonging to Thomas Michell and that all should be returned by 19 July to the almoner, who would repay any money that had been paid for them. Eventually the estates passed to Richard Michell, presumably upon payment of a fine to the Crown. No one saw fit to record a verdict of what caused Thomas Michell to kill his wife and sister-in-law, but disposal of his property certainly caused a stir in 1540.

From a much later century comes an intriguing case of a couple who each tried to murder the other. Was it a suicide pact? Or were the two so in tune that they chose the same means to attempt murder? The Shepton Mallet Gaol Records

report that at Bath on 2 April 1875 49-year-old Charles Maid-
ment and his wife Julia (34) were arrested and both charged
with feloniously administering to each other strychnine on 30
March. Both were found guilty and were sentenced to four
months hard labour.

There have been cases, of course, where excess affection
has led to death and the scaffold. Take Master Babb, for example. In 1613 he lived near Wambrook, outside Chard. He
proposed marriage to a widow living at Taunton and she refused him. He then hid himself in her brewhouse in the hope
of proposing again. When he appeared and popped the ques-
tion a second time she became so incensed that she hit him on
the head with a pewter candle-stick to reinforce her refusal.
This upset Master Babb so much that he produced a knife and
stabbed her sixteen times; then he put the knife in her hand to
give the appearance of suicide.

Even in those days sixteen cuts were fifteen too many to be
accepted as suicide. Mr Warre, a magistrate of Hestercombe
House, Taunton, ordered that everyone within a three mile
radius of the widow's home should assemble to touch the
body. It was widely believed at that time that if a murderer
touched the body of his victim, blood would flow. Master
Babb certainly believed the story; he ran off to avoid the con-
frontation, but eventually gave himself up and was tried at
Chard and sentenced to death. He died because the object of
his affections rejected him.

Another such case concerns poor Eliza Paine who died at
Worle near Weston-super-Mare when her sweetheart,
Charles Wakeley, got too excited while he was embracing
her. She told him he was going too far and to restrain himself,
which so annoyed Wakeley he drew a knife and plunged it
into her throat.

Then there was Joseph Wedlake, a farmer aged about 30.
He lived with his uncle on a farm at Winford between Barrow
Gurney and Chew Magna. In the same house lived Emma

Pearce, who was the niece of the uncle's wife. Wedlake fell deeply in love with Emma and for a short while it seemed she might be becoming fond of him. Then she met a man called Fletcher, and Wedlake was forgotten.

Wedlake was quick to take revenge.

One dark night he lay in wait behind a hedge armed with an axe. He knew that the two lovers had been together that evening and he intended to put a stop to their carryings on. He heard the footsteps of someone approaching; as the person neared the hedge he struck out with the axe – and found that he had killed the wrong one, a man called Mark Cox.

Emma and Fletcher had been to Winford Church that evening and were deep in conversation at the uncle's farm when Wedlake made his attack. Wedlake's brother laid information with the police, but Joseph said that had his brother not led the police to him, he would have confessed to the deed as his conscience had been troubling him. He was executed at Taunton on 21 May 1883, and on the same day George White is listed in the prison records as having been hanged for killing his wife. A year later the last hanging took place in Taunton when Charles Kite died for a murder he committed in Bath. After that Wilton Gaol closed and prisoners were sent to Shepton Mallet.

Some 7,000 sightseers attended John Beale's hanging in 1858. He had been out with his sweetheart, Charlotte Pugsley, in Leigh Woods, near Bristol. They had an argument and Beale slit Charlotte's throat. He died on 18 January, and the crowd who attended his execution was estimated to have been composed largely of women and gypsies. The executioner, a man named Calcraft (who was later to hang the Mannings), prevented a man from Bath touching the corpse. This man had a growth on his neck which he firmly believed would be cured by the touch of a hanged man. Calcraft never let him verify his belief, but a waxworks proprietor from Liverpool fared better – he was allowed to make a cast of the dead man's head for exhibition.

A small volume of poetry called *The Complaint or Night Thoughts*, written by Edward Young in 1742 (and memorable only for the line 'Procrastination is the thief of time'), is a poignant memento of a murder brought about possibly by despair at being found less than perfect by the lover. Written inside the front cover is: 'Wm White, who was executed at Bridgwater August 13, 1795 for shooting his sweetheart Maria Bally at Bath, gave this book to Sarah Briffett August 11, 1795.'

William White was an itinerant shoe-maker who was born at Beaconsfield in Buckinghamshire in 1773. He settled in Bath some time during 1793, where he met a well educated young woman named Maria Bally. Her father was a hairdresser, but she had been raised by her clergyman uncle and she was superior in status to White, and kept a day school for children. However, as the *Bath Journal* reported: '... the acquaintance betwixt them kindled into regard', and they planned to marry.

Then one day Maria found William had lied to her over something and she broke off the engagement. He twice went to her home but was unable to contact her. On the third day he went to the local pawnshop, operated by a man named Payne, and redeemed a pair of brass hand pistols that he had earlier bought in London to protect his property. Next he borrowed a clay pipe and melted a piece of lead that he had in his possession, used the bowl of the pipe to cast two bullets and loaded the pistols. He called in at a public house and drank a pint of strong beer and two glasses of brandy 'to which he was not accustomed.' Thus fortified he entered Maria's school on Corn Street. She was sitting bent over some needlework and twenty children were in the room with her.

White drew one pistol and shot Maria through the head. The children are reported as having run out of the room shouting, 'Murder, the man has murdered Mam.' He went out with them, shouting, 'I surrender myself to justice; I demand the justice of the law, for I have murdered her.' He handed over his pistols to one man and went quietly with another to the town prison from whence he was transferred to Ilchester Gaol (the Chaplain's Diary mentions him as acknowledging his guilt).

The next Assize following his committal was at Bridgwater, so William White was lodged at the Bridgwater town gaol where Samuel Briffitt was gaol keeper. Sarah Briffitt was presumably his daughter or his wife, and it was to her before his execution that White gave the book of poetry.

The book obviously meant a lot to White because, after spending 'half an hour in fervent prayer with the prison chaplain and another minister, he afterwards addressed the numerous concourse in a clear connected speech in which he quoted many passages from Dr Young's "Night Thoughts" and cautioned the younger part of his hearers not to trifle with each others feelings. The unhappy sufferer behaved with the greatest composure and resignation and seemed very penitent for the crime he had committed. The body after receiving some incisions from the surgeon [presumably to make sure White was quite dead] was delivered unto the friends of the deceased.' (*Bath Journal*, 17 August 1795.)

13
The Body on the Moors

All too often, the first that most people know of a criminal is after the deed has been committed. Rarely do you hear what lay behind it. Take William Burgess, for example. He was a heavy drinker and he was a widower. Had he been a heavy drinker before his wife died? Had that drinking contributed in any way towards her death? or was it her loss that led him to take comfort in the bottle? Whichever way round it was, his need for alcohol led him to the scaffold.

The story might be said to have begun in 1818 when John Knight, a wealthy businessman, bought vast tracts of the Royal Forest from the Crown with a view to developing agriculture on Exmoor and exploiting the mineral resources that were increasingly being sought by manufacturers at the height of the Industrial Revolution. So far as farming was concerned, Knight failed to take into account the height of the ground above sea level, the sparsity of soil and, most important, the impact of the climate on the growing of crops. Exmoor can suffer drought in summer and deep winter snow when the rest of the West Country is enjoying springlike weather.

John Knight's son Frederick took over from his father and through his agent set up several farms and leased them to tenants – of whom the locals said 'they arrived in their chaises and left in their tumbrils'. Knight was more interested in the industrial possibilities of the moor and in 1846 persuaded four local gentlemen (Richard Sleeman, surgeon, of Tavistock; Russell Richard, a lawyer from South Molton; John Lock, a developer, also of South Molton, and finally, another developer, Oliver Matthews of Molland) to join him in a consortium to exploit the mineral resources of the area. The agreement was that these four should employ at least six miners at a site known to hold a large deposit of copper. The partners would pay Knight 15% of the value of the ore removed, minus the cost of transporting it. When 200 tons had been removed, housing would then be built for the miners. Thus was founded Wheal Eliza Copper Mine at Cow Castle, near Simonsbath.

Flooding proved to be the mine's undoing and after a couple of years the venture was abandoned. The shaft filled with water and local children were warned by their parents to steer clear of the workings. Fortunately for the miners, the establishment of their little community had encouraged others to move into the area. The Church of England created the parish of Exmoor and built St Luke's Church and a vicarage at Simonsbath. William Henry Thornton, aged 27 and formerly of Countisbury and Lynton, was appointed curate in 1856 at an annual stipend of £150. He remained there until 1861 and, as he figured largely in the story of William Burgess, it is likely that the latter wished heartily that Parson Thornton had never been appointed to the living.

William Burgess, described as a labourer, lived with his wife and three children at Whitewater. Mrs Burgess died in 1857. The two older children, Tom and Emma, presented no problem to the widower; they were put into service at a North Molton farm, but Anna, or Hannah Maria, as she was referred to in the Coroner's Inquisition, was only about five years old and still too young to work. A local woman, Mrs Marley, who lived at Gallon House Cottage, agreed to give father and daughter lodging; her charge for the feeding and care of Anna was 2s 6d a week (12½p).

Burgess soon found his heavy drinking difficult to support on his wages (and probably at the back of his mind was the thought of how much it was costing him to keep little Anna). He did manage to raise some extra cash by persuading Parson

Thornton to write a brief for him. A 'brief' was the time-hon-
oured means by which poor illiterates sought help when they
had suffered financial loss by theft or fire, and by illness and
other means. The brief, which set out what had happened
and asking for a cash donation, was taken to the better-off
members of the community. By enlisting the support of a person of good repute, such as a clergyman, the petitioner was
lent credence. Burgess told Parson Thornton that he needed
to make good the loss of a pig and a pony, but he didn't tell
him that the loss had occurred several years before the curate
had come to Simonsbath. The brief was written for him and
Burgess made the rounds.

The curate was furious when he discovered the truth about
the time of the animals' death, and even greater was his anger
when he found that Burgess had spent the money collected
on liquor. Hell may have no fury like a woman scorned, but a
duped clergyman can come wondrously close, and Thornton
resolved to keep a close eye on Burgess in the future.

One Sunday in July 1858, Burgess told Mrs Marley that he
was taking Anna away to lodge with her grandmother at Porlock Weir. He collected up all her clothing – barely more than
one change of each item – and off they went. That evening he
returned home without the child and then, on the following
Thursday, he himself left Gallon House Cottage.

Not long after, someone noticed a small pile of clothing
smouldering on a fire behind the Gallon House Inn. Mrs Marley identified some scorched calico as belonging to Anna's
spare frock. This aroused suspicion. Parson Thornton
checked with the child's grandmother at Porlock Weir and
learned that Anna had not been left there on the previous
Sunday. The parson organised a search of the moors, and
then rode all the way to Curry Rivel to fetch the chief of police,
one Mr Jeffs. When the two men reached Simonsbath, the
searchers reported that a shallow grave had been found on
the moors, but there was no body.

At that time, although it was a hanging offence, sheep stealing was rife and the common practice was for moorland
sheep stealers to bury the carcase of the animal until they had
found a purchaser and then disinter and dispose of the body
in one operation. The grave was assumed to have possibly
been the work of such thieves.

The police and Parson Thornton thought it likely that
Burgess had taken passage by boat to South Wales – there
was much traffic across the Bristol Channel from ports such
as Porlock, Watchet and Lilstock. A search by the police at
Swansea found him and he was later discovered to have
reached there by a fishing vessel. Burgess was taken to Dulverton prison. Anna's boots were in his pocket, but when
questioned he refused to say where she was.

The search of the moors continued through the rest of July
and the whole of August, but still no body was found.
Burgess stubbornly refused to say where he had taken his
daughter and he knew that if he remained silent it would only
be a matter of time before he was freed. The magistrates were,
in fact, about to release him for lack of evidence when a man
came forward. He'd been reluctant to make a statement earlier because he had been engaged in nefarious activities (that
is to say, up to no good), but had been promised that no action
would be taken against him. He said that he had been near the
mine shaft at Wheal Eliza on the Tuesday night following
Anna's disappearance. He'd heard the sound of boots scrap-
ing on the ground and had hidden. Although it was a dark
night and he had seen nothing, he had sensed that someone
passed him going in the direction of the shaft. Later it was
learnt that on that Tuesday night Burgess had been in a pub
where two sheep stealers were talking. They had noticed a
newly dug grave on 'their patch' and reckoned another thief
had started operating in their area. They planned to go and
disinter the carcase and sell it to a buyer. Realising that he
must do something immediately, Burgess left the pub, went

Searching Wheal Eliza mine for the body of Anne Burgess.

along to where he had buried his daughter and dug up her body. Nothing was known of this at the time, but on the evidence the magistrates decided to make a final effort to find the whereabouts of little Anna Burgess.

It must have taken a great deal of courage to order the draining of Wheal Eliza mine; had there been no body, the Dulverton magistrates would have been held personally responsible for the cost of the operation. At that time farm labourers received 10/- (50p) for a week's work, and the lowest tender for the cost of pumping was £350. It took until the end of November to clear the water from the 360ft-deep shaft. When the bottom had been drained, a young man volunteered to go down, using a series of ladders. When he returned to the surface, pale from the exertion and from the lack of good fresh air at the bottom, he bore a tarpaulin-wrapped bundle. Inside that was a bag, and inside that bag was another bag containing the remains of Anna (Hannah) Maria Burgess, aged six.

A Coroner's Inquest was held before William Webber, the Monckton coroner at Exford on 4 December, 1858. William Burgess stood trial at the next Somerset Assizes in Taunton accused 'on the 25th day of July in the year of our Lord 1858 with force and arms ... feloniously, wilfully and of his malice aforethought did kill and murder Anna Maria Burgess against the peace of our said Lady the Queen, her Crown and Dignity.' He was found guilty and was hanged at Taunton Gaol on 4 January, 1859.

Recently further information has come to light concerning Burgess. According to David Foot, a West Country journalist and author, he was responsible also for the deaths of three other persons. When Mrs Burgess died, the widower sought to place Anna with the family of James Hayes, living at Withypool. James refused because his wife already had one small child and was shortly expecting another. This refusal so angered Burgess that he set fire to their house on the night of 13 January 1858. The young family escaped, but 63-year-old John Hayes, father of James, died along with two visitors named Shapland. All three are buried in Withypool churchyard. Burgess is said to have confessed to the crime while awaiting execution.

14
Bermondsey's Murder Most Foul

This case has been included because the perpetrator of the crime was a Somerset man and because his Somerset connections helped to trap him.

Journalists of 1849 had a field day when the news broke of the Bermondsey Horror – the mutilated remains of a man had been found on 17 August under the back kitchen floor at 3 Miniver Place. The house was owned by a man named Coleman, but at the time of the discovery it was unoccupied.

Some six months before, Coleman had let the house to a couple named Manning. The husband was a discharged railway servant, a guard with the Great Western Railway, who had been sacked following a series of robberies with a man named Nightingale on the trains he'd been supposed to be guarding. Later he was suspected of being involved in Post Office robberies for which a mail guard named Poole and another man had been transported.

The dead man was Patrick O'Connor, a gauger (exciseman) with the Customs Office at London Docks. O'Connor had been seen frequently with the Mannings and after he failed to return to his lodgings at 21 Greenwood Street, Mile End Road, the previous week, friends became worried about him and circulated handbills offering a £10 reward for his discovery. O'Connor was known to be fairly wealthy; it was thought some of his money came from usury – estimates of his fortune ranged from £4,000 to £20,000, but even the lower figure was a goodly amount for a man earning £300 a year. Meanwhile the Mannings had sold their furniture, vacated the house, and vanished.

PC 256 Henry Barnes of K Division was detailed to search

for the missing man. He went first to O'Connor's lodgings and found that all Patrick's boxes had been opened and emptied. The landlady remembered that Mrs Manning had been at the house on the Thursday night, 9 August, but she hadn't thought much of the fact as Maria Manning was frequently in and out of O'Connor's room. Then one of O'Connor's friends reported that upon meeting the missing man near Miniver Place on the Thursday he had learnt of O'Connor's invitation there for tea. Someone else said that he had heard Manning use threatening language toward O'Connor; Barnes began to fear foul play.

Together with PC Burton of M Division, he searched the house and decided to dig up the garden. That yielded nothing, but Barnes noticed that there was a dampness around the edge of one of the flagstones on the floor in the back kitchen. He and Burton lifted it and discovered the soil underneath was loose. They called for more help and on digging down about twelve inches, found the naked body of a man in a fairly advanced state of decomposition, with the face discoloured. O'Connor, however, had a remarkably thin and projecting chin, which, with his false teeth, served to identify him. For the first time ever, identification by means of false teeth was entered in court records when William Comley, a dentist practising at Osborne Street in Whitechapel, testified that he had sold O'Connor the teeth in June 1847.

A manhunt was on for the Mannings and from 18 August until the 30th, newspaper readers were able to follow the trail. It was alleged that at one time the dead man had been the lover of Maria Manning and that after their move to London, she had sought him out. Maria was described on the sheet offering £100 reward for information leading to her arrest as being 'aged 30, 5ft 7in in height, stout, of fresh complexion, long dark hair, good looking, with a scar on the right side of her chin extending towards the neck. Dresses very smartly, speaks broken English.' She had been born in Geneva; her father David De Roux had been a postmaster and before her marriage she was maid to the Duchess of Sutherland. She was described as a handsome, fine grown accomplished woman.

Her husband, according to the 'Wanted' poster, was 35 years old, 5ft 8 or 9in tall, stout, with a very fair and florid complexion, full bloated face, light hair, small sandy whiskers, light blue eyes and a peculiar form of eyelid at the corners and a large mouth. When the couple married at the parish church of St James, Westminster on 27 May, 1847, Frederick was described as a railway clerk, living at Taunton, son of Joseph Manning, gentleman.

Later investigation showed that Joseph Manning had been a sergeant in the Somerset militia who leased the tolls of Taunton market and some of the turnpikes. Frederick had been a favourite son and when the old man died he left him £400.

Manning appears to have had a chequered career. How long he was a railway guard is not known, but Hunt & Co's Directory of 1848 lists him as the proprietor of the White Hart Hotel in Taunton, a few yards south of today's Tudor Tavern. On the site of the White Hart is now a shoe shop, but E.F. Goldsworthy in his *Recollections of Taunton*, published in 1883, stated that it was one of only four inns in the town that had 'a light outside or inside their doors', so it was obviously one of the better class establishments. Incidentally, the White Hart was Kirke's headquarters at the time of the Bloody Assizes of Judge Jeffreys. One day, having invited his officers to an entertainment, Kirke commanded that thirty men were to be executed at the ancient market cross that stood at that time (1685) near the entrance to the White Hart. Glasses went round the table in three healths – one to the King, one to the Queen and the last to Judge Jeffreys, and with each toast, ten men died.

Frederick George Manning was born at Wiveliscombe, but his father was at one time licensee of The Bear in Taunton, so presumably it was Manning Snr who introduced the young man to the trade. Upon going to live in London, Fred again became a publican, this time in the neighbourhood of the Kingsland road, but as he was living at Miniver Place, it would seem to have been merely a lock-up establishment. Later it was reported that Manning claimed while they were living at the White Hart Maria left him, taking with her silver plate and money to the value of £400. This he gave as the reason why he could not pay his Somerset creditors, but they continued to press him and managed to extract 19/- in the £.

Reports began coming in of sightings of the Mannings from all over Britain – obviously their descriptions could be applied to quite a number of innocent citizens.

Neighbours of the couple at Miniver Place stated that some six weeks before the murder they had heard sounds, as though of digging, coming from the back kitchen, and a friend of O'Connor's said the dead man had told him he'd remarked on an excavation in the kitchen and been told by Manning that it was for the replacement of a drain. O'Connor had even teased Manning about the length of time it was taking to complete the job.

It is possible from the Central Criminal Court Minutes to follow all that led up to the murder of O'Connor. By then shorthand writers were employed at the Old Bailey and witnesses statements were taken down in full. The trial of the Mannings took place on 25 and 26 October 1849 in the Old Court in front of Lord Chief Justice Baron Pollock. William Massey, a medical student and lodger at 3 Miniver Place stated that Manning claimed O'Connor had shown Maria his will leaving all, or a considerable portion of his property to her. If Manning's claim were true, it was a powerful incentive to murder.

The couple laid their plans thoroughly, though they certainly left evidence aplenty for the police to follow later. Maria apparently wrote O'Connor a loving note inviting him for tea at 5.30pm on that fateful Wednesday. Before then, on a Monday toward the end of July, Frederick had visited a bricklayer's on Russell Street. He purchased six pennyworth of grey lime from Mary Wells, the bricklayer's daughter. He asked her which burnt the faster, white or grey, and said that he wanted it to kill slugs in the garden. On learning that there was no white lime in stock, he settled for the grey. Then Richard Welsh, an employee of Mr Wells, testified to having delivered a bushel of lime to Miniver Place which he'd emptied into a basket placed in the back kitchen of the house. Next day Maria Manning had given him a penny-ha'penny for his trouble. Manning next called upon a Mr Evans in King William Street to order a crowbar. Mr Evans sent his porter, William Danby, to deliver the tool. On the way Danby was met by Manning who complained that it was not wrapped, and was so much put out by the lack of covering that he insisted on the porter accompanying him back along Tooley Street until he found a stationer's where he could buy a sheet of brown paper.

Maria also went shopping. She visited an ironmongery belonging to a Mr Tooley on 8 August and looked at some shovels. William Cahill, the shopman, told the court that she first picked out a longer handled one, but on learning the price was three shillings she eventually settled for a short handled dust shovel costing 15d and had that delivered to her home. The stage was set.

When Maria had first re-established contact with him, the Mannings had intended that O'Connor should move in with them, but after only one night he moved out. Manning told the court that he and his wife had spent £30 furnishing the room for O'Connor and that she had shot him in the head because she felt he had let them down. Whatever their motive, after the shooting, the crowbar was used to fracture O'Connor's skull in sixteen places. Then the flagstones were lifted in the back kitchen floor and the body was put into the pit which the couple had prepared. The grey lime was spread, and the flagstones replaced. A 12-year-old girl, Ann Firman, took the stand to tell how on the Saturday before the discovery of the body she had seen Mrs Manning cleaning the windows of 3 Miniver Place and had offered to do some cleaning for her. Ann had hurt her hand so could not do all the work that was asked of her; she had cleaned the back kitchen, which was neither clean nor dirty, but had been unable to scrub out a basket that was on the floor and Maria Manning had done it herself.

Afterwards Maria left London. On the way to Euston Square station she called at London Bridge, which in those days was the terminus for the London & Brighton Railway Company. She deposited in the left luggage department two boxes addressed to 'Mrs Smith, Paris' and marked 'To be left till called for' and was issued with a cloakroom ticket. Later the boxes were opened and found to contain among other things, a bloodstained dress, a piece of muslin, and a toilet cover, also bloodstained. Frederick George's will was also there, along with a white tablecloth marked 'M. F. Manning, White Hart Hotel, Taunton'. Mrs Manning had then travelled by train to Edinburgh where, on the recommendation of a gentleman named Shaw, she had taken lodgings with a Mrs Hewatt at 25 Haddington Place, Leith Walk. With a surprising lack of imagination she still called herself 'Mrs Smith'.

Maria Manning wasn't long at large. Suspicion had been aroused when she took one of the stolen rail shares to a dealer in Edinburgh and tried to raise money on it. On 21 August Police Superintendent Richard John Moxey went to interview 'Mrs Smith' at her lodging and asked to examine her baggage. One of his men found a bill with 'F.G. Manning, The White Hart, Taunton' printed on it and he then arrested her, telling her he had reason to believe she was Maria Manning, wanted for the murder of Patrick O'Connor. Maria didn't deny her identity, but she accused Frederick of being a bad husband to her and drinking too much and said that O'Connor had been as a father to her. She was returned to London under police escort and lodged in

Horsemonger Lane Gaol.

Frederick George Manning had a longer run for his money. His steps were traced partly through the court and partly through the newspapers. The representative of a firm of stockbrokers testified that O'Connor had bought shares from them and said that later Manning claimed that he was Patrick O'Connor and tried to negotiate a transfer to himself by signing O'Connor's name. That certificate was entered as Exhibit No 1 in the trial. Then William Byford (no relation to my family), a hackney cab driver, told the court that he had had a fare from Charles Bainbridge's home, 14 Bermondsey Square on August 15 at 7.45am. He identified Manning as being his fare and said he remembered him particularly because he had directed him along a round-about route, up Bermondsey Street, along Tooley and up Union Street to Waterloo Station, the Southampton Railway terminus. He went about ¾ mile out of his way and the person paid 2/-. The man had a carpet bag and no other luggage.

Manning arrived in Southampton at 2pm and took up quarters at the Oxford Arms Inn near the railway station, just until midnight, when he caught the South Western Steam Packet Company's mail ship *The Despatch* for Jersey. Upon arrival at St Helier he went into town with an acquaintance named Turk and with him took a double room at the Navy Arms Inn. The two men explored the island together and then after a few days Turk departed, leaving the room to Manning. Turk later reported that Manning was very overbearing in his manner and he also drank heavily.

On Sunday the 19th Manning went to the Bath Hotel for the evening and became acquainted with the landlord's wife, Mrs Seward. He returned next day and nearly gave himself away in a discussion about the agent who supplied the Burnett's gin used by the hotel. The agent's name was Mann and Manning had first claimed to be a traveller for Burnett's gin. That same night he met a man from Taunton who knew him and who was on honeymoon on the island. The man turned

Prospect House, Jersey, where Manning was captured.

his head away but Manning realised he'd been seen. Mr Parsons, formerly a clerk of the Hampton race course also knew Manning and reported his presence.

A woman travelling on the *The Despatch* thought she recognised Manning and told her brother, a lodging house keeper where Manning had stayed for a few days in March 1849. The brother contacted John de H. Uttermarck, Crown Prosecutor of Guernsey, who in turn, on 22 August, wrote to the Lieutenant Governor of Jersey, Sir James Reynett. Another Tauntonian, a man named Trenchard, reported seeing Manning on the 19th in St Helier. It was decided to send Sergeant Langley, who had known the wanted man in Taunton, along with another police officer to Jersey.

Manning realised that the chase was getting close and he left the Navy Arms for a quieter spot on the island. He moved into Prospect House owned by an elderly couple named Bertan on Thursday 23 August. He stayed in his room all the time where he drank brandy, claiming that he was afraid of catching cholera and the brandy would help to ward it off. The old couple were trusting, but after a few days the brandy seller, a man named George Heulin, became suspicious of all the

drink being consumed. Mr Bertan was known to be abstemi-
ous. It wasn't long before two and two were put together – *The
Times* of 30 August announced the arrest of Manning;
Langley was the hero of the hour (he later received £10 reward for his part in the affair).

Frederick George and Maria Manning were found guilty
and sentenced to death on 26 October. Their execution took
place at 9am on Tuesday 13 November on the roof of Horsemonger Lane Gaol before a crowd estimated at being 30,000
strong. Between 400 and 500 policemen were drafted in to
control the spectators, who had been gathering since the previous day. The better off sightseers paid handsomely for
places in gardens, at windows and even on house tops in
Winter Terrace, which was reckoned to afford the best view.
Calcraft was the executioner and Manning went first, supported by two men and a chaplain; he appeared to be needing
that support. Maria Manning had tried to avoid execution on
the grounds that she was not British-born and therefore not
subject to this country's laws, but her marriage was deemed
to have bestowed citizenship. She asked to be blindfolded
and to have a black veil to cover her head and face so that the
crowd should not see her countenance. An hour later both
bodies were cut down and later that evening husband and
wife were buried in graves within the prison precincts.

Charles Dickens was present at the hanging and was so sic-
kened by the sight and the attitude of the crowd that he wrote
twice to *The Times* protesting at public hangings. His agitation
eventually led to the abolition of the practice. One final note:
in September 1938 the Libraries Committee of Southwark
Borough Council applied for permission to acquire the Mannings' gravestones. The two stones, marked with initials and
date of execution are preserved in the Cuming Museum, Wal-
worth Road, London, SE, where they are on permanent dis-
play (a free leaflet concerning the murder is available at the
museum).

15
Murderer of a King

Grant's Lane, situated between Langley and Ford to the north of Wiveliscombe was the scene of a murder in 1856. On the night of 23 December, a man named Hayes was awakened by the sound of a cart being driven at a gallop along the lane. The cart stopped by the gate at the entrance to his house and then someone ran off. Hayes took a lantern and went out to see just what had happened. He found in the cart the still-warm body of John Aplin, a 23-year-old farmhand who hailed from Cotton in the parish of Nettlecombe. Aplin was huddled up on the bottom of the cart and when Hayes examined him, he found his head had nearly been severed from his body.

Later investigation showed that Aplin had gone to Wiveliscombe on the morning of his death to draw some money for Christmas. He had spent the better part of the day drinking with Thomas Nation, a butcher's assistant with whom he had driven to the town. Witnesses later said that Aplin had shown Nation £5 that he had taken from his bank account. That evening Nation had insisted on accompanying the unfortunate young man on his journey home and it was assumed that it was he who persuaded Aplin to drive up Grant's Lane. A carpet bag belonging to Nation was found in the cart.

Thomas Nation was only 22; his father James, who lived in the village of Upton, had the reputation of being very miserly and of keeping his son extremely short of money. Earlier Thomas had stolen £18 from his father and had run off; he was traced and charged with theft, whereupon he handed back £17, having spent £1 and being unable to refund that amount. Thomas Nation also associated with gypsies, who in the mid-nineteenth century were regarded as thieves and rogues. Nation's chief comrade was young Stanley, son of a king of the gypsies who not long before had been found murdered in Devon. One day Thomas Nation rode on horseback behind young Stanley and the next day the latter complained of having been robbed of £27; naturally his companion claimed to have no knowledge of the money.

At his trial in Taunton on Friday, 3 April 1857, before Mr Justice Williams, Nation maintained his innocence in the murder of John Aplin but the evidence of thirty three witnesses, five of whom were called to testify, convinced the jury and he was found guilty. He was sentenced next day to be hanged and his body to be buried within the precincts of the prison. He was executed at Taunton at 8am on Tuesday, 21 April before a crowd estimated at being between 7,000 and 8,000. Among the spectators were many gypsies who made a point of attending because they were convinced that not only had Nation robbed young Stanley, but he was also the murderer of their king.

16
Family Affairs

Mary Ann Sealy was born in 1821 and her sister Faith in 1823. Along with several brothers and another sister they lived with their father William in what had once been a farmhouse at Pickney, near Kingston (now known as Kingston St Mary to distinguish it from the many other Kingstons in Britain). The house had been divided into two cottages and in the other half lived Betty Sealy, the 79-year-old aunt, or great aunt, of the girls. On 23 April 1843 William Sealy died. He had been suffering from stomach trouble, and was being treated by the local doctor, so his death aroused no undue suspicion. Neither of his older daughters was sorry to see the last of their father; he'd been a harsh man and had even thrashed them for going to dances. Both sisters had told the younger members of the family that they would be better off without him and, after his death, both went into service, although it would seem they continued to sleep at their old home. Their father's bedroom was let to a man named White, who, having been introduced, now disappears from the story.

The old lady frequently threatened to take her stick to the girls, so doubtless they didn't feel all that kindly towards her either. She became convinced that someone was stealing from her larder and complained that bread, cheese and bacon were being pilfered. Accordingly, early in December 1843, she hid in a closet near to the stairs in the hope of catching whoever was stealing her food. She may have discovered the identity of the thief, but she didn't live to say who it was. Her son and grandson, both called John Sealy, doubtless made suspicious by the absence of the old woman, broke into the house and found her stiff and cold body, clothed in her bonnet and cloak, seated on a chair in the closet. Her head was to one side, her tongue hanging out, and she had been strangled. A pocket of the dead woman's gown was partly torn and was seen to have once contained a heavy object that was octagonal in shape. At the Assizes, Betty Sealy, the old woman's daughter-in-law testified to having given her an octagonal bottle containing gin only a short while before.

Later, a half-pint octagonally-shaped bottle was found in Mary's room and because of a fault in the glass was identified as having belonged to the aunt. Scratches were noticed on Mary's hands. Searchers also found a movable floorboard in Mary's room through which it was possible to reach the aunt's pantry; this board was in such condition as to suggest that it had been used frequently. A verdict of wilful murder by Mary Sealy was returned at the Coroner's Inquest and she was committed to Wilton Gaol.

The death of old Betty Sealy stirred up questions about the death of Father William. His body was exhumed on 18 January 1844, and his organs were examined. The coroner issued a warrant charging Mary and Faith with murder by poisoning. The sisters were brought up for trial on 8 April 1844 at Taunton Assizes charged with patricide. The judge was Mr Justice Wightman and Mr Kinglake (later Serjeant-at-Law and Recorder of Bristol) was the defending lawyer, together with Mr Edwards. Mr Kinglake applied for separate trials and, this being granted, Faith was tried first.

In her evidence Faith accused Mary of the crime. She said she had seen her sister put arsenic powder into some salt fish bought at Taunton. Mary had also added the poison to the medicine prescribed by the doctor for their father's stomach complaint. Mr Sealy had complained at the taste of the fish and later that night his condition worsened and he died.

William Herapath, the analytical chemist from Bristol who appears in several of the accounts in this book, told the court in detail of his findings following the exhumation. Young Thomas Sealy (12), brothers John (14) and William (15) were followed by their sister Sarah aged 11, and all told the court how Faith and Mary grumbled about their father's strictness, and how they disobeyed him in the matter of returning home when told after a dance in the village.

Two young women who knew the Sealy sisters testified that Faith wanted arsenic to deal with rats, indeed Harriet Moman had gone with her to one shop and the pharmacist had refused to sell them the poison. Later Faith managed to persuade a 17-year-old apothecary's assistant in a shop belonging to a Mr Joyce to supply the powder and he told the court that he remarked as he did so that it was enough to kill a thousand men. Mr Joyce was warned in court that he should be more careful about what he allowed his assistants to sell.

In his summing up, Mr Wightman asked 1) whether William Sealy had died of arsenic poisoning? 2) was it administered by Faith?

The jury returned a verdict of Not Guilty and Faith was discharged; Mary was indicted for wilful murder of her father, but since the investigation had found Faith not guilty, the prosecution thought it right not to offer any evidence against Mary 'at that time', and she was acquitted. The crowds waiting outside the court room were so incensed by the verdict that to protect the sisters both were returned to prison, although technically Faith was free to leave.

Next day Mary was in court again, this time charged with killing Aunt Betty 'by squeezing and gripping and pressing upon her throat thereby choking or strangling her.' Mr Kinglake sought to prove that the old lady died from a fit and that the scratches on Mary's hand were circumstantial. According to him, bloodstains found on the doorpost of the closet came when the body was moved (despite being stiff and cold?). He submitted that the main evidence was also circumstantial and that it included several 'confessions' to fellow inmates in the prison. The 'motive' was to get hold of Mrs Sealy's club money – a sum of £8. The jury of twelve farmers and shopkeepers found Mary 'Not Guilty', but she had to join Faith once more in prison to safeguard their safety. An angry mob followed the van containing Mary right to the gaol gate.

The sisters were unable to return to their home. At first it was planned that they should make a new life for themselves in Canada, but eventually they emigrated to Australia and no-thing further is known of either. The *Taunton Courier* at the time reported that both Faith and Mary had had 'a marvellous escape' and referred to them as 'wretches' – obviously the court's decision was not one the writer of the editorial agreed with.

Old Betty Sealy was not the first, nor the last relative to be disposed of. Another aunt who suffered a similar fate was Sarah Waterman of Dundry, south of Bristol (in those days part of Somerset). The case was rather nasty; it involved two young men, Charles and Mathew Wedmore, and the victim was the wife of a Chelsea Pensioner, George Waterman. 75-year-old George had fought with the 9th Regiment of Foot in the Peninsular Campaign and was particularly proud of the Waterloo Medal that he was awarded following Napoleon's defeat. He and 73-year-old Sarah were reputed to have quite a bit of money stored away and they lived in reasonable com-fort in a house surrounded by about an acre of land. Their nearest neighbour was the village butcher, William Lovell, who lived about 150 yards away.

At the beginning of January 1861 a former policeman named John Keevil was approached by Charles Wedmore, a private on leave from the Marine Artillery. Wedmore asked whether Keevil knew William Wedmore or his uncle George Waterman. Keevil did, and offered to show him to the Water-man's home. The two men knocked on the door and, as Sarah was alone, she first called through the door to ask who was outside and upon being told 'John, the old policeman', let them in. George was at church that evening, but the two men sat and talked with Sarah, though she did not recognise Charles as her nephew. When they left, Keevil took Charles to William Wedmore's home, and from the reception they received it was obvious the two men were brothers.

On the night of 9 January, Mr Lovell noticed two strangers drinking at the Dundry Inn. Not long after he returned home, a bloodstained George Waterman staggered to the door with a horrifying story. Two men had come to the Waterman's home and knocked for admittance, calling out that one was John the Winford policeman. The door was opened and immediately one man hit George on the head with a long stick. They beat him up and forced him to take them around the house showing them where his money and valuables were. Then they took him downstairs and tied him up and told him to wait for a while before calling to his wife to free him. The old man asked that they should spare Sarah, and was told by Charles Wedmore that he had already put her to sleep.

Following their departure George managed to struggle free and seeing Sarah unconscious on the floor, made for the nearest house. William Lovell sent for the police and for the doctor and then had to help the old man back to his home. Sarah was beyond saving and died half-an-hour after the doctor arrived. George Waterman was not expected to live and his deposition was taken while he could still talk. He said that he did not know his attackers, but one was taller than the other and he would recognise them again if ever he saw them. His Waterloo Medal was missing along with two silver watches, his pistols, which he kept under his pillow fully loaded, and his keys.

Suspicion fell on Charles Wedmore and his companion, who from the description given by George, were identified as having been at the Dundry Inn. Next day's newspapers were full of the story of the vicious attack.

Jeremiah Jordan, landlord of the Thetis Frigate beer-house

in Tower Lane, Bristol, had a couple of early customers, one of whom (later identified as Mathew Wedmore) produced a silver watch and asked him to pawn it for him. Jordan sent his servant Mary Ann Colly to pledge the watch, and Wedmore handed him the ticket. Later that day Mrs Jordan sent to redeem the watch, which was then handed to the police. The brothers had wasted no time; on the same day the second watch was handed to a young woman named Mary Moxley, and she took it to a Mr Jacobs, another pawnbroker. She handed the ticket to the police and they retrieved the watch as evidence.

That evening, only 24 hours after the crime was committed, the police arrested Charles and Mathew Wedmore on Hotwell Road. They didn't go easily; both tried to run for it and when the police got too near, Charles turned and fired a pistol. He also dropped some keys, four of which were later found to fit locks in the Waterman household. At their trial held at Taunton, William Lovell and John Keevil were key witnesses, as was George Waterman, who had miraculously survived his ordeal. The old man identified the men, the watches and the pistols and the keys. The jury returned a verdict of guilty, although the defence had tried to persuade them that as they could not say who struck the fatal blow, both men should be acquitted. The judge was having none of that; he ruled that it didn't matter which did it if it could be shown that the two men both intended to rob and to commit violence if necessary to carry out the theft. The Wedmore brothers went to the gallows on 5 April 1861.

Almost three years before, in August 1858, a young man named John Baker Bucknell died in the same prison for killing his grandparents. On 14 April, 1858, *The Taunton Courier* carried an excited announcement on the editorial page telling readers that the Press had been 'Stopped to note A Shocking Murder At Creech St Michael'. News had just been received that morning that at a beer-house at Coombe, kept by a man

The Cottage Inn, near Creech St Michael.

named Bucknell, formerly a pig-jobber, a member of the household had discovered Mrs Bucknell in her bed with her throat cut and Mr Bucknell in the cellar with his skull beaten in. The next week's issue carried a more complete account, preceded by an apology for the inaccuracy of the first report.

John Bucknell (73) and his 76-year-old wife, Betsy, owned the Cottage Inn, and apart from selling cider and beer, Mr Bucknell did some farming and dealt in livestock, mainly pigs. Mrs Bucknell was helped by 12-year-old Ellen Jones who went each morning early to the house and performed various household tasks as well as serving beer and cider until about 8pm each night, when she returned to her home. The other member of the household was the couple's grandson, a young man named John Baker Bucknell, who had only six weeks before been released from Shepton Mallet Gaol after serving a year for breaking into a house in the village and stealing a silver watch. Before his imprisonment John Baker had lived with his grandparents; when he came out his grandfather refused to let him sleep at the cottage, although the lad (he was still only 20) still worked around the place and accompanied his grandfather to market.

On the night before the murder, Messrs Froom, Baker and Pain were at the Cottage Inn having a quiet drink with the landlord. Talk got round to pigs and pig dealing. Mr Bucknell said he intended taking some pigs next morning to Bridgwater, and he told his grandson to be round early so that they could be at market on time. Froom mentioned that he had some pigs to sell and the old man said he'd like to buy them, but perhaps Froom thought he hadn't the money and was afraid to trust him. Froom protested and Mr Bucknell said he'd got £40 in the house right then.

Next morning the village was in uproar. John Baker Bucknell claimed to have gone to the beer-house, knocked on the door and, unable to rouse his grandparents, had returned home to fetch his father. When neither man could get an answer, another man had been sent for and John Baker was instructed to fetch a ladder and look in through his grandparents' bedroom window. He came down, saying he could see nothing. Then the men forced the back door and John Baker said something was blocking the way. They got in through the front door and found the old man near the back door, dead, with a gunshot wound to the head. Upstairs his wife lay on the bed, her throat cut from chin to chest, the bedding soaked in blood.

A search revealed that only 6/- in silver was on Mr Bucknell. In a nearby straw rick was found a knife together with a bloodsoaked glove with 15s 6d in silver in the fingers. The knife was identical with one belonging to the grandson. Then PC Vickery, stationed at West Monkton, searched the pigsty some 20 yards from the house, and found two pair of sugar tongs, a £5 note on Stuckey's Bridgwater Bank, a pocket knife, a brooch, four sixpences, 1s 9d in coppers, part of a nutmeg, a letter and a key, all wrapped in a tartan patterned handkerchief. The key was found to fit the front door. Ellen Jones identified the handkerchief as one she had seen John Baker use many times.

The Coroner's Inquest, conducted by William Munckton, brought in a verdict of Wilful Murder. John Baker was arrested.

At the trial at the Assizes held at Wells on 9 August, William Reed, a rock blaster, told the court that the accused had asked him how touch rag was made for blasting, and when told it could be done either with salt petre or with rock powder, was then asked whether a gun could be fired with it. He told the young man 'yes, provided the powder was pounded down'. Next Baker asked whether the report from the rock powder would be as loud as that caused by the salt petre; 'no, it isn't as strong.' Baker then asked for some, saying he needed it to treat some fowls belonging to a Miss Morris. Reed estimated he'd given the accused about half an ounce; he'd asked how many hens were to be treated and when told a dozen, reckoned the amount he'd handed out originally wasn't enough, so he'd added a couple of thimblesful more. Miss Morris, called to the witness box, confirmed that she did indeed keep hens, but she had never asked the prisoner to do anything for her birds.

The keeper of a Bridgwater public house told the court that the accused had run up a considerable drinks bill at his establishment and had said that his grandfather would settle the account when next he was in town – presumably the presence of £40 in cash in the house had seemed a means of settling the debt, but I could find no mention of the money being found. The jury took only a quarter of an hour to find the accused guilty; after sentencing he was taken by van to Glastonbury and thence by train to Taunton, where he was once more admitted to the County Gaol. He was hanged there on 24 August.

John Baker Bucknell needed money to pay off debts, and he killed his grandparents to get it; Reginald Hinks seems to have wanted money to buy some of the luxuries of life that were becoming available in the Thirties, and he literally bumped off his father-in-law to get it. Had he been a little less helpful to the police, he just might have got away with murder; as it was he drew the full spotlight of suspicion on himself.

James Pullen, aged 85, was found dying beside a gas stove on 1 December 1933. He was described as a retired businessman and master tailor who lived in Englishcombe Lane, Bath. Questioned by the coroner, Mr C.S. Elwell, Mrs Hinks the dead man's daughter said that Mr Pullen had several times threatened to throw himself out of the upstairs window, and that he often played about with gas stoves. Her husband looked after the old man and on 30 November while her father was having his weekly bath, she had been putting her baby daughter to bed. Her husband had followed her downstairs to fetch clean clothing for Mr Pullen and had returned to the bathroom to find him under water. They managed to revive him. The next day he was found on the floor beside the gas stove with the oven door open and unlit gas pouring into the room.

Then Reginald Ivor Hinks testified. He said that Mr Pullen once employed two persons to look after him, but eventually the old man had decided that he, Hinks, could serve as his valet. He told the coroner that there were bruises on the head and these could be explained by the fact that he had pulled the old man out of the oven and had bumped his head on the floor in doing so. The two of them had been in the sitting room listening to the wireless since 5pm on 1 December. At about 7:10 the old man said he was going to the lavatory beyond the kitchen. Twenty five minutes later, Hinks, on his way to taking the baby a hot water bottle, pushed open the door dividing the hall from the kitchenette and saw Mr Pullen on the floor with his head in the oven.

Next to give evidence was Frederick Charles Strange of Claremont Terrace, Camden Road, Bath. He said he had cared for the old man from 24 January to 1 July 1933. He had once heard Mr Pullen say that he would like to cut his throat, but otherwise he wasn't suicidal. He reckoned though that the old chap needed constant attention.

The Pullen's former solicitor, James S. Carpenter, told the coroner that some property had been sold and Hinks had deposited the £900 received from the sale to pay for a house in his own name (in 1933 it was possible to buy a good sized semi-detached house near London for about £500). Hinks had suggested that there should be a deed of gift, but Mr Carpenter had objected as the young couple had not long been married. It transpired that Mrs Hinks had been previously married to a Mr Jeffreys who was the father of her child. The Hinks were married in March 1933. Nine days after their marriage Reginald Ivor had gone to the solicitor saying that Mr Pullen wanted to make a new will leaving everything to his daughter.

Then a wireless set dealer was called. He said that he had taken samples to the house in August 1933 and while there met the deceased whose mind seemed to be a complete blank. Hinks had confided in him that the old man had a great deal of property, couldn't last much longer and that when he died it would all belong to him. He also confided that Pullen was a nuisance and he wished he were out of the way. A nurse, Mrs Elizabeth Smith, said she'd been in the household since January to look after Mr Pullen, and she had never heard Hinks swear at him, although the old man did play with the gas taps. Despite Mrs Smith's evidence, on January 19 Reginald Ivor Hinks was charged with the wilful murder of James Pullen.

At the trial in February a doctor gave evidence that due to senile degeneration James Pullen did not even know of his wife's death, and yet Hinks had told the solicitor that Dr Scott Reid was of the opinion that the old man was fit to make a will. The solicitor brought a doctor with him to visit Pullen whom they found unable to understand any documents. The bruising on the back of the head of the body and Hinks's eagerness to explain it was regarded as strong evidence against him, as was also his efforts to take charge of the Pullen property. He was found guilty as charged and at 8am on 3 May 1934 was executed at Horfield Gaol, Bristol.

Finally, in this sordid saga of people disposing of unwanted relatives comes another from the 1930s. Sociologists today would probably say that both the death (and birth) of Dorothy Winifred Brewer came about because of poverty and social deprivation. She was 12 years and 9 months old when she died; she was also pregnant by her uncle, her mother's brother, who was also her father by an incestuous relationship (this did not come out until after everything had been cleared up). The Brewer family lived at Wrantage, outside Taunton, in the 1920s and early 30s.

The Brewers had five other children and so, in 1925, when she was 7 years old, Dorothy was sent to live with her maternal grandparents, Mr and Mrs Morse at nearby Slough Green, West Hatch. At least three sons were living with the old couple, and Dorothy was put to sleep in a bedroom also shared by her uncles Herbert and Harold. Three years later she was moved from that room and put in the same room as Uncle Fred, then aged 27.

Dorothy was a well built girl and could easily have passed for 16 or 17 by the time she was 12. In February 1933, her mother became suspicious about her condition and took her to a doctor who found that she was in an advanced state of pregnancy. It was left to Uncle Fred to tell her what was happening to her and he did so that night as he was tending to her hair before she went to bed, a service that he was accustomed to perform for her every evening.

The children at school, living close to the land as they did, had already been taunting Dorothy with their suspicions as to her condition and according to Fred Morse, next morning, 23 February, she began to cry and say that she didn't want to go to school and that she wanted to die. He arranged to meet her during his breakfast interval at the West Hatch lime quarry, at a crossroads some 200 yards from his place of work, and took her with him to Curry Mallet where he had to inspect some wire rabbit traps. They called in at the Bell Inn at Rock where Fred Morse ordered a glass of lemonade for Dorothy (or Mary, as he called her) and two packets of crisps plus a couple of pints of beer for himself. He then bought seven shillingsworth of rum, which the landlord's daughter thought strange as people usually bought it in quantities of a pint or half pint, and this was just over half a pint. She noticed that as he paid for the drink Morse was shaking.

Returning to Morse's first account of what happened, the couple walked to Park Farm and crossed the stream by a footbridge. He told Dorothy to wait for him in a nearby shed while he went to inspect the traps. When he returned three quarters of an hour later, she was gone and he noticed her footprints in the soft mud near the stream. He fell in while he was going along the bank looking for her, and so he went home to see whether she had returned. Old Mrs Morse stated that when her son returned home he was shaking, and he said he wished he knew where the girl was. When she asked him if he'd done anything to her, he denied it vehemently. The police were informed and in the early hours of the morning Morse was taken to Taunton Police Station. He told his story and was returned to West Hatch.

Next day Morse was out with the police searching for Dorothy and they soon found her body, half-submerged in a stream and caught in the low-lying branches of an overhanging tree. A search of the shed produced a watch, bought by Morse for the girl, but often used by him. Outside the shed a cigarette card was found and not far away was an empty bottle that had contained rum. Fred was then invited to write his account of what happened. The pathologist at Taunton Hospital reported that there were no marks of violence on the girl's body and only slight bruising on the cheeks.

Four days later, the well known Home Office pathologist, Sir Bernard Spillsbury, was consulted by phone and came down to Somerset to examine the body. He found that there were traces of an alcoholic beverage present in the stomach, but could not identify which spirit it was – an assistant said that it smelt like rum. The police returned to West Hatch, they required another statement from Morse.

Chief Inspector Bennett and Detective Sergeant Salisbury of Scotland Yard questioned Morse for several hours, and eventually he signed a statement.

In it he admitted that he had seduced his niece and said that Dorothy and he had agreed to a suicide pact. He had given her some rum to drink beforehand and they had both jumped into the stream. Dorothy had clung to his arm and he had tried to get her to the bank, but he was too weak and she had been caught by the current and carried away. Morse was taken by car from Taunton to Ilminster where, before two magistrates he was charged with the wilful murder of Dorothy Winifred Brewer – at that time the survivor of a suicide pact was deemed to be guilty of the murder of the other party.

At the trial at the Somerset Assizes, held at Wells before Mr Justice Goddard on June 7, J.G. Trapnell, KC was the prosecutor and J.D. Casswell the defending counsel. Casswell felt the only defence was to somehow attack the veracity of the second statement, and he thought he saw a way when Chief Inspector Bennett testified to the court that he had never seen the first statement made by Morse. Since in normal procedure the first thing CID officers would want to know was how far local police had got in their enquiries, Casswell again asked the inspector whether he had seen that first statement and was told 'no'. Then the inspector claimed that he had seen Morse writing the incriminating statement and that he was leaning over his shoulder as the man was writing it. Casswell recalled the Somerset police inspector who testified that the handwriting of the second statement signed by Morse was, in fact, his own. Bennett's testimony had been showed to be flawed, and Casswell felt that this might help his client.

Morse, however, proved to be a sullen witness. He returned to his original story, but then damaged his own case when he told the court that he had found Dorothy's body on the day that she went into the stream, but had said nothing to the police. The judge asked why he had not told anyone that before, but Morse remained silent. The jury retired and brought in a verdict of guilty, and furthermore they expressly said it was not murder as the result of the suicide pact. The judge sentenced him to hang. On 16 June Messrs Alms and Young, the Taunton solicitors, gave notice of appeal against the death sentence on the grounds that the possibility of an accident should have been considered. Morse had, after all, told the landlord of the Bell Inn where he was taking the girl and, furthermore, the judge did not put to the jury a suggestion made by the defence that Dorothy had been sick and might have died from shock at the fall into freezing water. The appeal was dismissed.

Fred Morse, quarryman, was hanged by the famous executioner Pierrepoint on 25 July 1933 at Bristol Gaol.

17
Unlawful Killing

Four men were tried for the murder of PC Nathaniel Cox in 1876; one was set free and the other three spent twenty four years in penal servitude because, while it was known that one of them had killed a policeman, all three stuck together and none would incriminate another.

Nathaniel Cox was the village policeman at East Coker; he was 37 years old at the time of his death, and an experienced member of the police force. He'd been on duty with the West Coker policeman, a man named Henry Stacey, on the night of 16 November. The following day was the start of the Yeovil Fair when crowds of farmers and people from outlying areas (which included among them many vagrants and ne'er-do-wells, especially poachers) were expected to converge on the town. Traditionally the police had always had their hands full during the fair and the Chief Constable had ordered an especial crackdown on poachers that year. To forestall trouble he told the patrolling officers to operate in pairs. Stacey was younger than Cox, and had been only three years in the force and possibly it was to fortify his courage that he had had a drink before going on duty that night. After he had met with his partner both men had a drink in several pubs while on duty – much was to be made of those drinks by the defence at the subsequent trial at Taunton.

According to Stacey's evidence, he and Cox were at Netherton around 10pm when they heard a horse-drawn cart coming towards them with three men on board, and with possibly a fourth lying on the floor of the cart. Both parties greeted the other, and the policemen allowed the cart to pass unimpeded. Almost two hours later the policemen were en-

joying a glass of ale at the home of a farmer named Squibb
when they heard the sound of the cart returning. This time
one man was driving, three were walking and the cart appeared to be full. The constables left their drinks and quietly
followed the party. As the cart slowed to begin the sharp haul
up a hill on Netherton Lane, Cox went forward and stopped
it, asking the men what the cart contained. Upon being told it
was none of his business, he said that he and Stacey intended
to search it. Stacey, at the back of the cart trying to see what
the contents were, then heard the sound of a blow and ran to
the front to find Cox sprawled on the road. In turn he was
attacked and knocked unconscious. When he came to, face
down in the ditch, the men and cart had gone. There was no
sign of Cox. Stacey managed to stagger to Darvill Farm (Dar-
vole on today's maps) and waken its owner Henry Marsh.

Marsh, when he heard the story, fetched two of his labourers who lived nearby and between them they assembled
lamps and a cart and went back to Netherton Lane (west of
the A37 Yeovil-Dorchester road) to search for PC Cox. They
found him dead, with his staff broken, some 70yards from
where he had stopped the cart. His skull had been smashed in
and his brain was protruding on the left side of the head, consistent with having been repeatedly kicked. The men loaded
the corpse onto the cart and took it to a pub called the New
Inn at East Coker and then sent for the local doctor. Stacey
himself was badly injured and spent several weeks in hospital with severe concussion, compounded no doubt by the exertions of fetching help and then returning to the scene of the
crime.

The police had little evidence to go on, the darkness prevented Stacey from seeing clearly the men involved, but a
family named Hutchings disappeared from nearby
Hardington and handbills were circulated giving a verbal description of the wanted men, a father and his two adult sons.
They were known poachers and had had frequent brushes

with the law. The fourth man, Charles Baker of West Coker, was soon apprehended and taken to Yeovil and charged with murder. The other three were nowhere to be found. A reward of £100 was offered for information that would lead to their arrest.

Here, the newspaper reports are at variance with information that turned up in the Shepton Mallet Gaol Records. According to the newspapers, not long after the reward was offered, toward the end of January, James Vagg of West Coker, a butcher by trade, drove up to Yeovil Police Station to hand over George Hutchings and his son Giles, who he claimed to have found on the road not far from Hardington. He was after the £100 reward, but the police wanted Peter Hutchings as well. Acting on a premonition of the deputy chief constable's, Yeovil police searched Vagg's premises and lo and behold, there was Peter. All three men were in poor condition; none was liked in their home village and in the adjacent villages, so they had not been able to turn for help to sympathetic supporters. Vagg was charged with harbouring a wanted man, but with the help of a number of influential people who testified on his behalf, he was discharged and went back to his butchering.

There's no mention of a Vagg in the Gaol Records but, following the admission of Charles Baker (able to read, unable to write, 36-years-old, labourer) on 5 January, 1877, and of George (58), Giles (32) and Peter (25) Hutchings (all described as labourers and admitted 20 January) is an entry for James Richards, aged 50 and George Richards, aged 45. Both are described as dealers with previous records for stealing; this time they were charged with harbouring the three Hutchings. The Richards brothers were called upon to find sureties to appear at the next Assizes if called upon.

The charge against the Hutchings is merely recorded as 'wilful murder' – no mention of the victim's name, nor of the fact that he was a policeman. There is a tendency to think of

IN MEMORY OF
NATHANIEL COX
A POLICE CONSTABLE OF THIS
COUNTY WHO WAS KILLED WHILST
IN THE DISCHARGE OF HIS DUTY
ON THE NIGHT OF NOVEMBER 16 1876
AGED 37
IN THE HOUR OF DEATH, AND IN THE DAY
OF JUDGMENT, GOOD LORD DELIVER US.

The memorial to Police Constable Nathaniel Cox.

assaults on the police as being a modern phenomenon, but it was a common reason for imprisonment in the nineteenth century, if Shepton's Gaol Records are anything to go by.

The Hutchings and Baker were committed for trial at the Assizes held at Taunton in March. The courtroom was packed, and outside was a large crowd. The defence counsel laboured the point that the policemen had both had a considerable amount to drink on the night of 16 November, and he also suggested that the four accused were on lawful business on that night and that Cox had no business stopping the cart. W. Molesworth St Aubyn told the jury they had to be able to point the finger at the man who killed Cox or else they must acquit all four of murder. The judge in his summing up said he felt that all or some of the prisoners were involved in the killing, but as to what exactly happened no one could say. This summing up served only to confuse the jury more.

After only three-quarters-of-an-hour deliberation they returned a verdict of manslaughter by all four defendants. Baker interjected before the judge pronounced sentence to say that the old man had not left the cart. The judge granted George Hutchings a Free Pardon and the Gaol Records note that he died on 26 April, 1877; the following day, the other three men were transferred to Pentonville Prison, each to begin serving 24 years of penal servitude.

The disgust of the crowd, especially those who knew the Cox family (the constable and his wife had four young children), when they heard that the accused were escaping with their lives (though penal servitude at that time was certainly unpleasant) caused many an angry letter to be written to editors of both local and national newspapers. George Hutchings, had he lived, would have been shunned by the community, and fortunately for the other three, before their 24 years was completed, they had been mainly forgotten by their fellow villagers.